# THE
# RIGHT
# TO
# KNOW
## Censorship
## in America

# THE RIGHT TO KNOW
# Censorship in America

ROBERT A. LISTON

Franklin Watts, Inc., New York · 1973

Library of Congress Cataloging in Publication Data

Liston, Robert A
    The right to know; censorship in America.
    Bibliography: p.
    1. Censorship—United States.  2. Obscenity (Law)
—United States.   3. Executive privilege (Government
information)—United States.   I. Title.
KF4775.L58              344'.73'0531              73-1266
ISBN 0-531-02612-4

Design by Diana Hrisinko

*To*
**STAN DRAKE**
*and*
**TOM SHOEMAKER**

# Contents

# Introduction

I am not writing a book advocating censorship. As a writer of facts and ideas I simply cannot. As an individual who has just returned to the United States after living for years in the totalitarian nation of Spain, which practices rigorous censorship, I cannot. No thoughtful person who has ever lived under severe censorship can ever responsibly advocate it.

Nor am I writing a book advocating total freedom of expression and information, which is to say the absence of any form of censorship. As an individual, a father, a concerned citizen, I simply cannot say that there are *no* words, expressions, no ideas that should be forbidden, which is to say *censored*. Our existence, both as a society of mankind and as a nation, depends upon *some* restraint of information and ideas.

What I have attempted to do is write a book exposing these two conflicting ideas to rational consideration. These two polar concepts are the root of both America's long history of censorship and the courageous efforts to oppose it. These two opposing ideas strike at the essential meaning of freedom in our society. Part of our much-observed American malaise lies in our confusion over what should be censored and by whom.

No answer lies here. I have neither the knowledge, wisdom, nor arrogance to attempt to provide one. I am simply trying to set forth that information and those ideas that may assist you in arriving at your own conclusion.

I have divided the book into two parts, censorship of obscenity and censorship of information, touching briefly upon other matters such as intellectual freedom and the right to privacy. The greater part of the book considers the censorship of obscenity, but not because it is the more important issue. In considering censorship as it relates to obscenity and pornography, however, we can explore the problems of censorship whatever the nature of the material.

I am indebted to Miss Connie Jenkins, a senior student, and Miss Thelma Bumbaugh, librarian at my alma mater, Hiram College in Ohio, for making pertinent books available to me; my daughter Cynthia who researched some specific items for me; John Noble, Richard Gilman, Carole Paskins, and Tom Shoemaker; and most especially Mrs. Eleanor R. Seagraves of Washington, D.C., who once again produced reams of highly pertinent and invaluable material for my use. I would like also to express a general "thanks" to all those people, too numerous to mention, in newspapers, magazines, and publishing houses who over the years instructed me in censorship and the joys of freedom of expression.

R. A. L.
*Trumbull, Connecticut*
*July, 1972*

# PART I

# Censorship of Obscenity

# CHAPTER 1
# The Censorship Controversy

● CITIZENS of an American community launched a campaign to take the "filth" out of the public library. Self-appointed, vigilante committees removed from the shelves over six thousand books, including Herman Melville's *Moby Dick,* Ernest Hemingway's *Through the River and into the Trees,* Aldous Huxley's *Brave New World,* and works by William Faulkner, James T. Farrell, Somerset Maugham, John O'Hara, C. S. Forester, John Steinbeck, James Michener, John Dos Passos, Eugene O'Neill, Erskine Caldwell, D. H. Lawrence, George Orwell, and George Bernard Shaw. With the enthusiastic permission of the town's mayor, the books were publicly burned.

● A thirteen-year-old seventh grade girl visited a neighborhood movie theater to see a widely acclaimed film. She witnessed a prolonged rape scene and she was so greatly upset by what she had seen that she had difficulty sleeping that night.

● In Washington, D.C., a subcommittee of the Senate Foreign Relations Committee asked the Defense Department for a list of foreign military bases where nuclear weapons are stored. The request was refused on the grounds of protecting national security. The committee insisted, maintaining it was studying United States security commitments to other nations. Ultimately, the Defense Department did brief the committee with the understanding that only one transcript be made of the testimony and it be kept in the State Department.

• Also in Washington, a secret memorandum indicating that the Nixon administration favored Pakistan in the 1972 India-Pakistan war was leaked to a newspaper columnist who published excerpts from it. Administration officials reacted with dismay, feeling they had to be extremely careful of what they said in the future and of what they put into writing. Representatives of foreign governments expressed reservations about their ability to speak frankly in the nation's capital.

These four incidents, all based upon recent items in the news, are reported here because they illustrate the problem of censorship in America.

Opponents of censorship cite book burnings, the difficulties even Congress has in finding out what the United States government is doing, and attempts to silence unpopular opinions as examples of the dangers of censorship. Such actions, they maintain, violate the Bill of Rights and pose a danger to America by choking off valuable ideas that might help the nation solve its problems.

Advocates of censorship cite the dangerous effects of explicit sex and violence upon children, the need for secrecy in conducting some of the nation's affairs, and the need of society to protect itself against those who would destroy it as examples of why the nation must practice some censorship. Without censorship, they claim, America may lose the very freedoms the Constitution seeks to protect.

These examples were chosen for two other reasons. First, they illustrate the major areas of censorship this book will cover—obscenity and freedom of information. Second, they illustrate extreme situations that cause Americans to fear both censorship and its absence. By dealing in emotional extremes that prey upon fear, we frequently make rational discussion of the censorship problem difficult, if not impossible.

*Congress shall make no law* respecting an establishment of religion, or prohibiting the free exercise thereof; or *abridging the freedom of speech, or of the press;* or the right of the people peaceably to assemble, and to petition the Government for a redress of grievances.

This is the First Amendment to the United States Constitution, the cardinal principle of the Bill of Rights, the basic protection of the American people against tyrants, well-meant and otherwise, who would deprive them of their liberty.

I have italicized that portion of the amendment that most directly affects censorship. "Congress shall make no law . . . abridging the freedom of speech, or of the press . . ." That principle was held so dear by our forefathers of the late eighteenth century that it was listed first among the rights the people demanded before they agreed to ratify the Constitution that established our form of government.

That statement has echoed through history since it was written in 1789. It literally inspired millions throughout the world to immigrate to the United States to obtain the liberty promised in those words. Even today, despite the denigration of America and Americans throughout much of the world, those fourteen words stand for the best in America. We are constantly judged by the rest of the world for our ability to render true meaning to those words. Our courts, our legislatures, our elected officials, and large numbers of our citizens have courageously fought for about two hundred years against those who would deny to anyone the freedom offered by the First Amendment.

But it is also true that the United States has a long history of censorship. Few Americans realize how wide a variety of censorship is practiced today throughout the United States. Some form of censorship, both legal and illegal, voluntary and coerced, is applied to nearly everything we read in books, magazines, and newspapers, to what we hear on radio, and to what we both see and hear on television and in motion pictures. Much of this censorship is insidious and little known. Only the smallest portion of the censorship is based on national, state, or local laws. Most of the censorship is private and carries with it an aura of intimidation. A member of Congress makes a speech denouncing the "sex and violence" on television, and the broadcast industry, because it is regulated by the federal government, seeks ways to censor its own programming. The motion picture industry concocts a code for rating its films that will alert the public to the type of audience that ought to view them. Librarians omit certain books from the catalog or hide them on less obvious shelves. Publishers of books, magazines, and newspapers decide what the public ought to know or read. Businessmen, sometimes under the threat of government intervention, self-censor their production and advertising to avoid affronting those who might possibly object to their products or the sale of them. The police raid a book store, movie house, or theater, prohibiting certain means of expression, even though they know the raid is illegal. The police realize they can "get away with" the raid and effect censorship through intimidation. A citizens' group, acting as a censor, carries on a private campaign to keep what it considers objectional writings and films out of its community. The group offers rewards to cooperating stores and theaters, and boycotts those who do not cooperate.

Very little of such activity is performed in the name of censorship. Because of our respect for the First Amendment freedoms, even the most active censors tend to consider "censorship" a dirty word. A number of apparently more acceptable euphemisms are used instead. Some are "regulation" or "self-regulation"; "good taste"; "classification," "national security," or "vital interests."

At this point it is important to ask a question: How can we honor freedom of expression at the same time as we are seeking to censor it? That question, I believe, strikes at the heart of the censorship problem in America, for all of us want a certain amount of both freedom of expression and censorship of it.

Few, if any, thoughtful Americans believe the First Amendment guarantees of speech and press are absolute.

There are rational limits. The classic example is that no man has the right to cry "fire" in a crowded theater when there is no fire, thereby causing people to rush for the exits where they might be trampled and hurt.

A more pertinent example might be that no person has an inalienable right to telephone a school or airline or any public place and state that there is a bomb in the area, knowing there is none. The expense, inconvenience, hysteria, and danger to the people involved make this an exercise in "free" speech that benefits no one.

There are a significant number of such examples. The guarantee of free speech does not give a person the right to tie up a party telephone line with idle chatter to prevent a person from calling a doctor in an emergency or reporting a fire. No person has an inalienable right to use the local newspaper to summon people to meet at a certain time and place for the purpose of burning down the local courthouse, police station, or anything else.

The reader can undoubtedly add to such a list. The point must be obvious. Society, the community of man, must be protected against speech, both oral and written, which is malicious and harmful. No person, First Amendment or no First Amendment, has a perfect right to say or publish anything that comes into his head.

Therein lies the problem that opens the door to censorship. What is malicious and harmful to society? Is it harmful and malicious to publish photographs of individuals engaged in bizarre sexual activities? Or to print what had been thought to be confidential information about government and business activities? Or to give "aid and comfort" to an enemy engaged in armed conflict with the United States? Or to reveal publicly the private activities and attitudes of a government official, business enterprise, private citizen, or anyone else? Or to publish ideas that incite people to violence? Or to suggest that we overthrow our form of government and adopt some other system?

These are but a few of the very serious and practical matters that lead to confusion among Americans over the conflict between First Amendment freedoms and censorship. This confusion leads all the way to the Supreme Court, the nine justices of which frequently wrestle with the insistent and often opposing demands of freedom and censorship.

Whenever Americans seek to apply censorship (calling it regulation or whatever), they open a Pandora's box of problems. First, what is to be censored? The malicious and harmful to be sure, but what precisely falls in that category?

Second, who is to be the censor, deciding what other Americans are to see, hear, feel, know, and be influenced by?

Third, to what extent is there a risk that censorship, no matter how well meaning, may frustrate the development of those innovative ideas that America so desperately needs in order to cope with such problems as war, overpopulation, pollution, declining national resources, urban blight, education, poverty, mass transit, and materialism at the expense of the quality of life?

Fourth, does censorship, in whatever guise it is applied, diminish the quality of freedom in America? Does censorship make more difficult the achievement of the national goal of creating a truly free society?

We have wrestled with such problems throughout our history. The current hue and cry in the press about obscenity in books, magazines, and movies and about government abuse or misuse of security classifications, such as "top secret" to conceal information from Congress and the people, indicates that the problems are very much with us today.

The problems of censorship, difficult to deal with at best, are worsened by a high level of rhetoric. Those who would censor and those who abhor censorship often carry around an image of the other that makes it very difficult even to discuss the possibility of compromise. Censors are viewed as rigid, terribly conservative, unhappy, unintelligent, sexually frustrated, chauvinistic in their patriotism, and utterly "out of step with the times." Those who oppose censorship are viewed as "wild-eyed radicals," nihilists, libertines, licentious, immoral to say the least, unpatriotic and even anti-American, intellectuals of the "egghead" variety, and bent on destruction of this country and what it stands for.

Needless to say, such attitudes are a great deal less than helpful. There are many thoughtful, concerned individuals who believe both in censorship and in the need to keep it to a minimum. There are concerned advocates of both views who offer appealing, well-thought-out views that cannot be idly dismissed. Censorship is a problem and will remain so until we become a nation of angels.

It seems that we move closer to the solution of the problem when we remove the mindless, unhelpful rhetoric and approach the opposing viewpoints in an unemotional, rational manner. We may not be able to eliminate, but we can hopefully minimize the sensationalism that pervades the discussion of these controversial issues.

As a beginning, let us attack head-on the most controversial issue, the censorship of obscenity.

CHAPTER 2
# What Is Obscene?

THE biggest problem in writing about or discussing obscenity or pornography—indeed, in censoring it if one wishes to—is to define it. A well-meaning person might be wholeheartedly for obscenity or against it, if only he knew for sure what it was.

It seems that pornography or "filth" or "smut," as it is variously called by those who disapprove of whatever it is, lies, like beauty, in the eye of the beholder. There are about as many definitions of pornography as there are individuals with the courage to attempt defining it.

One citizen, apparently seriously, objected to receiving advertisements in the mail from leading American department stores that depicted articles of female undergarments. This individual, at least, construed the Sears, Roebuck catalog as pornographic.

Perhaps equally distant, but in another direction, from the usual definitions of obscenity, is the view of the Reverend Howard Moody, pastor of Judson Memorial Church in New York City. Writing in *Christianity and Crisis* in 1965, the Reverend Moody said, "The true profanity against God is to refuse to take him seriously; the truly 'dirty' word is the one used to deny and to denigrate the humanness of another person." He then offered this definition of obscenity:

> For Christians the truly obscene ought not to be a slick paper nudity, nor the vulgarities of dirty old or young literati. . . . What is obscene is that material, whether sexual or not, that has as its basic motivation and purpose the degradation, debasement and dehumanizing of persons. The dirtiest word in the English language is . . . the word *nigger* from the sneering lips of a Bull Connor [former police commissioner in Birmingham, Alabama]. Obscenity ought to be much closer to the Biblical definition of blasphemy against God and man. . . .
>
> I do not conceive that a picture is "dirty" because sex is its dominant theme. . . . The "lewdest" pictures of all—more obscene than all the tawdry products of the "smut industry" —are the pictures of Dachau, the ovens, and the grotesque pile of human corpses." *

Thus, in the eyes of the Reverend Moody, pornography is not limited to sex, which is the key element in nearly every other definition.

As part of its studies, the research staff of the Commission on Obscenity and Pornography asked ninety-one female junior college students from the Washington, D.C., area to list some magazines they had read and considered pornographic. One-third of them named *Playboy* magazine and nearly half mentioned various "confession" and "romance" type magazines. All needless to say, are fixtures on newsstands.

The junior college students were asked to name books they had read that they considered pornographic. Of the ninety-one young women, forty named *Candy* and thirteen *Harrod Experiment*. Named by from four to nine of the young women were *Fanny Hill, The Carpetbaggers, Adventurers, Myra Breckinridge, Valley of the Dolls, Lady Chatterley's Lover,*

* Dachau was one of the concentration camps in Nazi Germany in World War II where large numbers of Jews and others were murdered.

*Exhibitionist, Tropic of Cancer.* The titles could be a distillation of the "best seller" list for the nineteen-sixties.

Elsewhere in its research, the commission asked 625 students from eight well-known colleges and universities in Westchester County, New York, to give a definition of what they considered to be pornography in literature, films, and other forms of communication. The following table is the result reported by the commission:

|  | Males | Females | Total |
|---|---|---|---|
| Filth, animal level sex, degraded | 17% | 20% | 19% |
| Nudity, the sex act, sexual excitement | 8 | 23 | 18 |
| Exploitation of sex | 19 | 17 | 18 |
| Bad taste, not artistic, what minors should not see | 9 | 6 | 7 |
| No plot, meaning, or purpose | 4 | 3 | 3 |
| No moral or social value | — | 3 | 2 |
| Only in the mind | 4 | — | 1 |

Of some interest is that 5 percent of the students said they could not define what they considered pornographic, 2 percent said "nothing is" and a full 25 percent either did not bother to or could not answer the question.

Clearly, there is a good bit of confusion and indecision among college students when they are asked to define obscenity. What of the experts? How do the professionals studying pornography define it?

A research team headed by Morris E. Massey of the University of Colorado studied pornography in Denver for the Commission on Obscenity and Pornography. For the purposes of its study, the Massey team differentiated five types of written or pictorial pornography. Class A involved "people engaged in a sex act with full exposure of all private organs." Class B included "people engaged in sex play with private sex organs not in contact but fully exposed," or "people engaged in a sex act, but no private sex organs exposed to viewer." Class C consisted of "people with all private sex organs fully exposed, but no sex action shown or implied." These were considered "medical type" exposures. Class D included fully nude people, for example nudist camp scenes. Class E were the "girlie" type magazines such as *Playboy, Mr., Male, Sir.*

Such classifications are doubtlessly sufficiently scientific but they are a long way from itemizing the activities offered for sale, if not in Denver, then in New York, San Francisco, Detroit, and other cities. For an appropriate fee, usually deposited as separate coins in an "arcade type" device, scenes of masturbation, copulation, and other sexual acts may be seen. If sufficient money is at hand, one can enter "adult" theaters and witness full-color films of various sexual activities and organs. It is even possible in the United States to go a good bit farther than that. For sufficient money, a person can purchase time alone in a "photography" studio with a nude model who will pose in whatever position is desired. The fee also includes a camera and film. A person can also witness live performances of two individuals performing a variety of sex acts and even, until the show was raided by New York police, performances of a woman engaging in the sex act with three different animals.

With such activities we are surely moving closer to a definition of pornography that would win wide public acceptance. What of the public prosecutors who are charged with upholding obscenity laws and defending public morals? The commission queried nearly five hundred prosecutors about the various problems they faced in enforcing obscenity laws. One clear-cut result of the survey was that the larger the city, the greater the pornography problem.

Among prosecutors in cities of 500,000 or more, large numbers said the following were "cause for concern" in their communities: erotic films shown in theaters (78 percent), erotic paperback books (76 percent), magazines featuring models with genitals or pubic hair exposed (78 percent), homosexual magazines (63 percent), girlie magazines (58 percent), nudist magazines (51 percent), erotic films for sale or rental and underground newspapers (37 percent each).

These may be a "cause for concern" in America's cities, but the simple fact they are sold in the public marketplaces indicates that concern or no, they are not considered pornographic, at least in the eyes of the law.

Is nothing obscene or pornographic? As matters have developed in the United States, the Supreme Court in Washington is the final arbiter in the argument over what is obscene. In effect, the high court has become a nine-member board of censors. A considerable number of books, magazines, and films have gone before the Court to be judged either obscene or not obscene. With few exceptions, as we shall see somewhat later, the justices have disagreed strongly about these matters.

The justices have indicated that they have little taste for their assumed role. To avoid it, they have attempted to define pornography so that police, prosecutors, and lower court judges can decide what is or is not pornographic. To be obscene, the court has ruled that material must be:

1. *Utterly* without redeeming social importance; and
2. Dominated by a theme that appeals to prurient interests if contemporary national community standards are applied; and
3. Patently offensive because it affronts contemporary community standards relating to sexual matters.

The tests are so broad as to make hardly anything obscene, a fact both decried by those who would censor pornography and applauded by those opposed to such censorship.

The difficulties with such a definition of obscenity were pointed out by the late Justice Hugo Black in a dissenting opinion in 1966. He said no human beings, serving as judges or jurors, could be expected to decide what appealed to prurient interest on any basis that promised any kind of uniformity. He said such a decision would "depend to a large extent upon the judge's or juror's personality, habits, inclinations, attitudes and other individual characteristics . . ."

As for the second standard that pornography is patently

offensive to contemporary community standards, Justice Black said he was left with a feeling of uncertainty as to whether the "community standards" were "world-wide, nation-wide, section-wide, state-wide, county-wide, precinct- or township-wide." Even if definite areas were mentioned he felt that different standards would be applied throughout the country. "So here again the guilt or innocence of a defendant charged with obscenity must depend in the final analysis upon the personal judgment and attitudes of particular individuals and the place where the trial is held."

As to the requirement that pornography be "utterly without redeeming social value," Justice Black said this seemed to him "to be as uncertain, if not even more uncertain, than is the unknown substance of the Milky Way." He added:

> Whether a particular treatment of a particular subject is with or without social value in this evolving, dynamic society of ours is a question upon which no uniform agreement could possibly be reached among politicians, statesmen, professors, philosophers, scientists, religious groups or any other type of group.

We have, thus, great difficulty in arriving at a legal and consensual definition of obscenity or pornography. Perhaps all that can be said for certain in this large and varied nation is that obscenity lies in the eye of the beholder.

Yet, it is perhaps possible to assert that pornography exists. *Something* is probably obscene to everyone, engendering such reactions as fear, loathing, disgust, whether it be to unwanted pictorial displays of female underwear or sexual acts between a woman and animals.

Despite the possibilities for disagreement over what constitutes pornography, it seems to be possible to agree on a list of some of the *characteristics* of pornography.

1. *The subject matter relates to sex.* The views of the Reverend Moody that pornography includes the blasphemous, violent, and dehumanizing is novel and pen-

etrating, but the history of censorship and the law both indicate that obscenity and pornography relate to sex.

2. *It is a public display of sexual activity.* Throughout history sexual intercourse and related activities have been a private act between two individuals who consider themselves alone. At the most, sexual activity has occurred among a small, homogeneous group. Pornography would seem to be an exception to this, involving literary, pictorial, or live sexual acts before total strangers. Such a statement should not be construed to include necking and similar displays of affection, including sexual intercourse of the type that has occurred at rock festivals and similar gatherings. There are those who would label such activity as pornography, but it seems to me to lack the other characteristics of it. Such public displays of sex might be said to involve a rather loose definition of privacy or even be exhibitionism.

3. *A monetary fee is involved.* Everyone pays to see pornography. There is a price attached to the book, magazine, photographs, playing cards, stag film, movie admission or whatever. A number of "porno" shops now charge a dollar just to enter and browse. The admission fee is subtracted from the price of what is subsequently purchased. Even if a person is able to look at a friend's pornographic material for nothing, an original price was still paid for the material. The payment of money to look at pornography makes it at least a first cousin to prostitution.

4. *There is an absence of love.* Pornography depicts exclusively loveless sex. There is no genuine evidence of emotional involvement between the participants. Such characteristics of love as thoughtfulness, tenderness, helpfulness, protectiveness, and unselfishness are nowhere in sight.

5. *Interest in pornography is a phenomenon of males.* Research by the staff of the national Commission on Obscenity and Pornography showed that the customers of

porno shops, theaters, and such places are overwhelmingly, if not exclusively, male. The content of pornography is calculated to appeal to men rather than women. Studies by the commission and others indicated that few if any women are sexually aroused by photographs of naked men or sexual acts. Those photos of male "muscle boys" in porno shops are for the benefit of homosexuals. Virtually every study indicates that sexual material must include elements of romance and love to appeal to women.

6. *Pornography exploits women.* The dominant theme of pornography is male mastery over women. As writer Stanley Kauffman aptly described it, "Performed pornography is an exercise in the humiliation of women. . . . The men who are involved in porno performance . . . are not being so humiliated. They are treated as masters, usually, and the performances are done for their satisfaction. Those male performers are vicars for the almost entirely male audience. . . . Performed porno makes every man a sultan." Even in the "Class E" "girlie" magazines, such as *Playboy,* females are depicted as willingly naked to bring pleasure to males. In pornography, women are seminal vessels and nothing else.

7. *Pornography engenders guilt.* Researchers for the national commission made extensive observations of porno patrons. Most came into shops or theaters singly and avoided other patrons. There was an absence of conversation. No one asked for help in locating particular material, as in a conventional book store or library. Furtive glances were common. Great efforts were made to hide the material being looked at. Perusal stopped when the patron observed that someone was looking at him. In theaters, the patrons tend to sit off by themselves, if possible keeping an empty seat between themselves and other viewers. It is a common practice for the lights to be kept off for a few minutes

after the performance ends to permit patrons to leave unseen. If such observed behavior does not indicate guilt feelings, it certainly does reveal that the patrons of pornography are not terribly proud of their actions.

8. *The sensibilities of at least some people are affronted.* There may be wide disagreement concerning what people find offensive and disgusting, but one of the characteristics of pornography, of whatever variety, is that it is offensive to somebody, generally to quite a lot of people. At the very least, that which is obscene is making a degrading public spectacle out of what most human beings consider a private expression of some type of love or involvement.

9. *Pornography involves the arts and demeans them.* By its very nature, pornography must make use of writing, painting, sculpture, photography, the theatrical arts, even dance. One of the characteristics of pornography, as well as a major complaint about it, is that the use made of these arts is uniformly dreadful. In recent years efforts have been made to improve pornography artistically through better photography, more attractive models, and by offering at least some semblance of a plot and purpose. But it is still extremely difficult to think of a single pornographic contribution to the arts. If there were any, the material would not be considered pornographic under current legal definitions.

It may be said that none of these characteristics of pornography is wrong or evil, *per se.* With a little effort it would be possible to produce a qualified expert or at least a line of reasonable argument to commend every one of these characteristics.

Yet, Americans, however they define it, have long considered pornography an evil and sought to censor it. A look at this history will be illuminating.

# CHAPTER 3
# The Golden Age of Censorship

SHOULD the obscene and pornographic be censored in America? That is a central question of this book. We can contribute to the answer by considering the censorship that has taken place in the past.

There has been a lot of it. In 213 B.C. Chinese emperor Tsin Chi Hwangti, the builder of the Great Wall of China, ordered all books destroyed except those concerning science, medicine, and agriculture.

Of even greater loss to mankind was the repeated sacking and burning of the famed library at Alexandria, Egypt, by the Romans, Arabs, and Christians. Some estimate that as many as 700,000 volumes were destroyed over the centuries and with them most of the accumulated knowledge of the ancients. Even today man is handicapped by the loss of what the ancients knew and had written.

Perhaps every civilized nation could cite a history of book burnings and censorship. Unlike modern censorship, most of the bannings and burnings were not based on sexual content. Censorship in ancient times and well into the eighteenth and nineteenth centuries sought to eliminate that literature that was deemed blasphemous to the Christian, Moslem, or other religion, or which was considered dangerous to a king, kingdom, or some other state government. We still practice a good bit of this type of censorship in America, as we shall see in Part II.

The earliest censorship case in America was in Philadelphia in 1815. A man named Jesse Sharpless was convicted of exhibiting a "certain lewd, wicked, scandalous, infamous, and obscene painting, representing a man in an obscene, impudent, and indecent posture with a woman, to the manifest corruption and subversion of youth, and other citizens. . . " It is interesting that the judges reached their decision without ever viewing the offending painting for fear of "wounding" their eyes.

Even more fascinating is the first court case challenging obscenity in a book. The work in question was *Fanny Hill* by John Cleland, which had been published in England in 1740. It was published in America under the title *Memoirs of a Woman of Pleasure,* which may indicate that our forefathers also had their minds on the cash register. The book, which is considered to be rather well written and illustrative of the eighteenth-century English prose style, describes in considerable detail the activities and adventures of an English prostitute.

In 1821, Chief Judge Isaac Parker of the Massachusetts Supreme Court banned *Fanny Hill* as "lewd, wicked, scandalous, infamous, and obscene. . . ."—again without reading it.

And thus it remained until 1966, when the United States Supreme Court ruled that the book was not obscene. Compounding the irony was the fact the Supreme Court decision overruled a four to three split decision made in 1965 by the highest court in Massachusetts that *Fanny Hill* violated every test of obscenity. Among the judges of Massachusetts, at least, there was agreement, spanning 134 years, that *Fanny Hill* was obscene.

Censorship was not considered a major problem in colonial America or in the early days of the republic. England and other European countries practiced it on a larger scale than did America. The United States had a pronounced history of religious freedom and since most censorship in Europe was in the name of religion, the colonists and founders were more determined than ever to avoid censorship as an infringement on religious freedom.

There was plenty of the obscene or prurient around, as *Fanny Hill* indicates, but the populace seemed unconcerned. The illiteracy rate was high. Books were largely a luxury reserved for the rich and educated. The church was a powerful influence. The exigencies of taming a harsh land gave little time for pondering the sexually bizarre.

As the publishing of *Fanny Hill* in 1821 indicates, these conditions began to change. More books of wider variety began to be published and concerned citizens began to see them as a threat to public morals. The first anti-indecency law was passed in Vermont in 1821. Connecticut was second and other states followed. Fear of the obscene was only part of the rationale for these laws. North as well as South feared that if such sexual material got into the hands of blacks, both free and slave, it might lead to rebellion, sexual license, and a lot of other unwanted difficulties.

Censorship of the obscene was not practiced widely until after the Civil War. The man who brought it to the public's attention was Anthony Comstock. Born in New Canaan, Connecticut, in 1844, Comstock grew up in a highly religious home. While serving in the Union Army during the Civil War he was affronted by the bawdy stories and "oaths" uttered in the barracks. After the war, he clerked in his home village and then in New York City. Again he was affronted by the interest of other men in "erotic books and pictures."

Comstock's ire was first directed at saloonkeepers who remained open on Sunday, disobeying the law. He called a policeman to close them, but the policeman refused to act. Determined to be a "good citizen," Comstock brought charges against the saloonkeepers before the police commissioner.

Comstock's singleminded devotion to upholding the law

came at a time when there were new laws on the books banning obscenity. In 1865, Congress had passed a law calling for fines and jail sentences for anyone who sent obscene materials through the mails. But the Post Office Department was not given the right to censor the mails. The recipient of the obscene material had to complain before prosecution could begin. Comstock quickly made a name for himself as just such a complainant.

He was further aided by a New York State law, passed in 1868, which sought to suppress obscene literature by prosecuting dealers who sold it. Comstock spent all his spare time seeing that dealers in what he deemed obscene materials were arrested and prosecuted.

Comstock's activities coincided with a period of moral fervor in the United States. The press, authors, clergymen, and ordinary citizens were obsessed with the notion that the "impure" should be removed from society. The first canon of this doctrine was that nothing "impure" should befall the eyes of a woman, for she was judged a "lady" on her ability to keep away from such impurities. She had an important ally in Anthony Comstock.

New, tougher laws were passed. Comstock joined with the YMCA to found the Committee for the Suppression of Vice. The committee was quickly chartered by the State of New York as the Society for the Suppression of Vice, with Comstock as its agent. Some of the wealthiest and most prominent men in New York (J. Pierpont Morgan, William E. Dodge, Samuel Colgate) supported him.

Comstock soon went "national." Congress enacted what became known as the "Comstock law." It declared nonmailable "every obscene, lewd, lascivious, or filthy book, pamphlet, picture, paper, letter, writing, print, or other publication of an indecent character." Banned, too, were all articles, drugs, medicine designed for "preventing conception or producing abortion." Comstock was appointed special agent for the Post Office with police power.

Comstock threw himself into his work with unbounded

zeal. In 1874 he reported that in a period of two years his society had seized 130,000 pounds of bound books, along with 60,300 "articles made of rubber for immoral purposes."

He and his cohorts raided book stores, publishing houses, and gambling dens, seizing articles they deemed obscene or iniquitous and destroying them. Houses of prostitution were raided and the women who inhabited them were "rescued." The "arm of the law" as wielded by Comstock was very long. By the time he retired in 1915 amid the plaudits of the nation, he estimated that in his "fight against obscenity" he had convicted enough persons to fill a passenger train of sixty-one coaches and destroyed over 160 tons of obscene literature.

Comstock was not just a man of action. He delivered many speeches against books that caused lust. "Lust defiles the body," he said, "debauches the imagination, corrupts the will, destroys the memory, sears the conscience, hardens the heart and damns the soul."

There were many who agreed with him. Antiobscenity societies were founded in cities throughout the nation. All vied to be more militant than Comstock.

But the Comstocks eventually became objects of ridicule, first among a small element of the population, then among the dominant group. When Comstock died in 1915, the *New Republic* grudgingly admitted he had done a "vast amount of good" but had also "conspicuously made an ass of himself." It is difficult to believe that such an "offensive" word could have been printed in Comstock's heyday a few years before.

There was ample evidence of the decline of Comstock-style censorship. In 1905 Comstock prosecuted a production of George Bernard Shaw's new play, *Mrs. Warren's Profession,* which was prostitution. Comstock lost. A New York court ruled the play did not violate the state obscenity statute.

Shortly before his death, Comstock railed against a "rotten" book entitled *Hagar Revelly.* Written by Daniel Carson Goodman, a physician, the book told of two sisters, one pure and one definitely not, and the happiness and misery that came to each. It was a morality play. Comstock considered it obscene and prosecuted the publisher of the book. Comstock won in the lower court but lost in the Federal Court of Appeals.

In the more permissive era of the "roaring twenties," the decline in the effectiveness of the New York Society, now headed by John S. Summer, continued. Increasing numbers of its prosecutions began to fail in the courts, and the victorious "smut peddlers" began to sue the society for damages as a result of malicious prosecution—and to win the suits.

Among the key cases the New York censors lost was one against a bookstore clerk named Raymond D. Halsey, who sold an agent of the society a copy of *Mademoiselle de Maupin* by French author Théophile Gautier. The book was deemed not obscene. The case was farreaching in that the court considered the book as a whole, rather than a few isolated paragraphs from it, as had been the practice previously. The judges also listened to testimony from literary experts concerning the quality of the work and the reputation of Gautier.

The New York Society fought back, determining that more stringent legislation was necessary if the tide of unfavorable court decisions was to be reversed. Something called the "clean books" legislation was prepared and sent to the New York legislature. It sought to put "teeth" into the existing obscenity statute by permitting an obscenity indictment to be based on *any* part of a book. And, only the offensive part could be submitted in evidence. Moreover, books deemed "filthy" and "disgusting" by the censors could be suppressed, even if they did not deal with sex. Finally, trial in obscenity cases had to be by jury and introduction of expert testimony was expressly forbidden. Clearly, the New York vice society was endeavoring to have the legislators legalize exactly what the courts were saying was illegal.

The bill almost passed. A powerful campaign was mounted for it. Even publishers and librarians joined in the clean books crusade. But the reaction set in. Other publishers, authors, and politicians began to criticize censorship in general and the methods of the vice society in particular. A second attempt was made to get the bill passed, but it got nowhere.

The last straw for the vice society came in 1929. The previous year a book entitled *The Well of Loneliness* by English author Radclyffe Hall was published in America. It had been banned in Britain, but a small American publisher, Covici-Friede, published it in the United States even though it dealt with a most sensitive subject, lesbianism. Critics loved the book, praising its honesty and sensitivity. It is considered a classic on the subject to this day. Obscenity crusader John Summer immediately purchased the book and police followed quickly with an arrest.

The case dragged through the court, but the book was declared to be not obscene. Two effects of the decision were important and long-lasting. The court decision established that a book could not be declared obscene solely on the basis of its theme. More significantly, the book sold 100,000 copies within a year. Clearly, there was a lot of money to be made by being banned. The lesson has not been lost on authors and publishers to this day.

The demise of the New York Society for the Suppression of Vice after more than sixty years of energetic censorship was paralleled by the decline of similar types of censorship societies in other cities. The last to fall into ill-repute was the famed Watch and Ward Society of Boston, which made the term "banned in Boston" an article of national scorn and a certain way to sell books.

Watch and Ward had a quieter, more subtle and thus more effective method of censorship than was used in New York. The more conservative and polished Bostonians did not rant and rave and engage in wholesale prosecutions. They established a Booksellers' Committee consisting of several Watch and Warders and the more responsible booksellers. The committee read and judged all new books, then either approved or disapproved them for sale in Boston. If disapproved, all bookstores were alerted that they were not to sell the book. If they did they would be prosecuted. For a long time, the method was highly effective. Booksellers, since they participated in the decisions, could not truly criticize the method. There was a distinct tendency on the sellers' part not to stock the book and thereby avoid trouble.

The man credited with destroying the system was Henry L. Mencken, the Baltimore author, professional iconoclast, and publisher of the *American Mercury* magazine. Mencken, who disliked all forms of censorship, carried on a generous campaign in the magazine against the Watch and Ward Society. The Boston censors were less than enthralled by the derogatory publicity they received from Mencken.

It all came to a head in 1926, when *American Mercury* published a story called "Hatrack." It told of a small-town prostitute who was publicly abused, but privately honored by the community's better citizens. The Watch and Ward Society banned the issue of the magazine in which it appeared. The censorship was heeded by all but one dealer who sold a copy of the magazine. He was arrested.

Mencken was undaunted. He traveled to Boston and before a crowd of 5,000 gathered on the Boston Commons he sold, with obvious relish, a copy of the magazine to J. Frank Chase, chairman of the Watch and Ward Society. Mencken was promptly arrested.

The death knell for the Watch and Warders came, first, when Mencken was found innocent of selling obscenity, and, second, when he won a court injunction prohibiting the Watch and Ward Society and news dealers from harrassing the *American Mercury*. In granting the injunction, the judge termed the group's censorship methods "clearly illegal." The Watch and Ward Society did not disappear for a long time, but it became much less effective.

As the older censorship groups declined in public esteem and effectiveness, new groups, many of them representing organized religions, took their place, but the climate of censorship for the written word was past. The golden age of censorship was over.

There were still court cases, but the censors lost more and more of them. A classic example involved James Joyce's *Ulysses,* published in America in 1933. Rather than obscene, the judge found the book to be a "sincere and serious attempt to devise a new literary method for the observation and description of mankind."

An attempt was made in Congress in 1929 to tighten the postal and customs laws against obscenity. Particular targets were the new pulp "confession" magazines such as *True Confessions* and *Modern Romances.* Rather than arresting and badgering dealers, censorship groups sought to stop distribution of such "filth" by having the post office rescind their second-class mailing privileges. Customs officials were hounded to stop the importation of foreign books deemed obscene. At one point in 1928, the post office and Customs Bureau united to draw up a list of 700 books that could not be imported into the United States or sent through the mails.

The censorship issue came before Congress. Its lengthy debate was perhaps a mirror of the conflicting viewpoints about censorship throughout the nation. In the end, Congress liberalized the customs law. Customs officials were not permitted to precensor a book. Their decisions were subject to review by the courts. Books were to be judged as a whole, not just by isolated passages. Some books could be admitted, obscene or no, because they were considered classics.

The more liberal attitudes toward censorship have been growing more or less steadily ever since. Most important to our considerations here is this question: What caused the change in attitudes toward censorship?

There were several things. First, the excesses of the censors. When Comstock managed to stop publication of Walt Whitman's *Leaves of Grass* as obscene, it struck a lot of people as a bit ridiculous. Many other banned books fell into the same category. People who had read them or managed to read them despite the censorship realized the ban was silly. It required a twisted mind to read obscenity into many items of classical literature.

Second, the censorship began to strike people as irrational. To give an example of the times, if it was granted that prostitution was a public evil that ought to be eradicated, how could an enlightened citizenry go about doing so if all books containing information and ideas about the problem were banned? And the same logic could be applied to a number of other sexual problems.

Third, widespread, vigilante censorship became rather difficult to justify in terms of the First Amendment guarantees of freedom of speech and press. That there was more censorship than freedom was obvious.

Fourth, some authors, publishers, and book dealers, began to stand and fight for First Amendment freedoms and against censorship. The legality of censorship was questioned in the courts and the authors and publishers began to win, particularly when they appealed to higher courts.

Fifth, and probably most important, public attitudes began to change. What had been obscene in the 1870s simply no longer was in the 1920s. Styles of dress changed. Women began to work, became more independent, won the vote, and began to enjoy greater freedom. Rather obviously, they did not need to be protected from the "impure" quite so much and maybe some of the impure was fun and not very harmful. The books, censored or no, magazines, movies, and radio, not to forget the automobile, changed the nation's attitudes and customs. It is axiomatic that in America no law can really be enforced if the majority of the people do not want it to be enforced. The demise of censorship of the Comstock variety was perhaps more than anything a reflection of public attitudes.

But this leads to an important question. What changed public attitudes toward sex and obscenity? To what extent did books contribute to the freer attitudes? It is these questions that are discussed in Chapter 4.

# CHAPTER 4
# Heather and Yon-
# Cheesecake to
# Nudity

EVEN during the Comstock era, but especially after the 1920s, the better novelists, both foreign and American, began to treat sex as a human condition, a fit and proper subject for description, discussion, and plot development. They wrote of it matter-of-factly. They felt no compulsion to moralize. Sex was part of life, and they believed the novelist's task was to portray and enhance the meaning of life.

A celebrated example occurred in Ernest Hemingway's *For Whom The Bell Tolls,* written in 1940. The book is about an incident that took place during the Spanish Civil War. It tells of the efforts of a group of Spanish republicans, the losing side in the war, and one American, Robert Jordan, to destroy an important bridge. The book contains a love scene between Jordan and Maria, a Spanish girl who had been sexually brutalized by enemy soldiers.

Jordan and Maria meet in a field of heather and make love. Because Hemingway was a master writer—some would say the best of modern times—he was able to fill the short scene with compassion, tenderness, and passion based upon love. He saw the love as a human condition that flowered amid the desperation, loneliness, and hopelessness of this forsaken band of human beings. What he did not say spoke volumes because of the little he did say. His description of the lovemaking was the antithesis of explicitness. Using perfectly proper, anything but vulgar English words, he conveyed the rhythm of sexual intercourse. At its climax "the earth moved."

Hemingway was concerned with human beings. He gave no descriptions of sexual organs or processes. Nor did he moralize over the fact Jordan and Maria were unmarried. Sin, damnation, effects upon society were not even considered.

Few people at the time and hardly anyone since considered the scene obscene. To do so is to say that human love is obscene. Yet, the love scene between Jordan and Maria is a classic. Totally lacking in explicitness and vulgarity, it remains one of the most erotic love scenes ever penned.

The problem was, and is, that not all writers are Ernest Hemingway or William Faulkner or John Steinbeck or Pearl Buck, to name America's recent Nobel Prize winning novelists. Sex all too often became not a part of life, but an object of life. Books came to be written, not to portray man, but to portray sex. Descriptions became increasingly explicit. Characters could not just feel desire or lust or love as a human condition. Pages had to be devoted to just what those feelings were and what provoked them and what actions were taken about them.

For a time, authors "closed the bedroom door," leaving the reader to understand that a seduction had occurred and that it had been wonderfully satisfying. Then, particularly with the rise of the paperback publishing industry, the bedroom door began to remain open and readers were permitted to witness, feel, and hopefully experience vicariously.

The sheer volume of such books drove authors and publishers in the direction of the bizarre. Human bodies became phenomenal and characters' capacity for sexual activity monumental. Forms of what had been considered perversion were rendered commonplace. Sadomasochism such as flagellation or whipping for sexual purposes, bestiality, male homosexu-

ality, lesbianism, group sex, wife swapping, child molesting,
and whatever else cunning minds could think up seemed "just
naturally" to follow. And even when the paperbacks were relatively tame, the covers, vying for luridness, suggested the opposite.

A feature of such books was that sex was highly desirable.
It was uniformly an ecstatic experience. In fact authors, in
truly amazing displays of inventiveness, sought to make each
of the many experiences more ecstatic than the one before.
Sex between adults, whether consenting or not, was portrayed
as having its own redeeming virtue. Sex for sex's sake. Ethical
and moral issues virtually disappeared.

Serious novelists such as John O'Hara, Vladimir Nabo-
kov, John Updike, Norman Mailer, Henry Miller, Erskine
Caldwell, and Philip Roth, continued to write about sex and
sexual subjects with artistry and serious purpose, but their
very daring and critical and financial success spawned a host
of less talented imitators. At best these lesser authors dwelled
upon sexual themes and strung the sexual episodes together
with a plot, preferably one filled with action, violence, sensationalism, and fictionalized "inside" revelations about famous,
barely disguised celebrities.

A parallel advance from the intriguing to the explicit and
possibly pornographic occurred among magazines. In the
nineteen-twenties, thirties, and forties, America's most respected and popular magazines, along with newspapers, made
generous use of "pin-ups" or "cheesecake" photographs. Even
the nation's most conservative advertisers were devoted to the
notion that a photograph of a pretty woman helped to sell
their products.

"Cheesecake" was respectable. It consisted of a pretty
face, a happy smile, and an attractive figure. Apparel consisted of a bathing suit, either one-piece or two-piece (the bi-
kini was not yet popular) as fashion dictated, a tight sweater, a
nontransparent negligee or nightgown, or a "low cut" evening
gown. Greater nudity than that was taboo. For bare breasts
and bottoms one had to purchase nudist magazines or photo-

graphic or art magazines. Only with the greatest rarity did respectable magazines such as *Life* or *Look* print nude photos, and then only under the guise of art. Even such an unabashed "men's" magazine as *Esquire* limited itself to the more tantalizing cheesecake and drawings.

The step from photographic suggestiveness to nudity was taken by *Playboy* magazine in 1953. In its first issue it ran a nude photograph of actress Marilyn Monroe, which covered three pages as a foldout. The magazine was an instant success, and every monthly issue since has contained a nude foldout. The magazine literally bulges with bare bosoms and buttocks.

Hugh Hefner, the founder and publisher of the magazine, did his very best to make nudity respectable. The centerfold "playmates," as they were called, were uniformly young, nubile, and innocent looking. They were photographed with painstaking care (one photograph might take weeks), by expert photographers, and shown in poses that were suggestive, but that avoided any connotation of sexual activity. Pubic areas were not revealed and no man appeared in the nude photos.

The nudes were always identified, if only with pseudonyms. They had hometowns, careers, and families, all of which were depicted in nonnude photographs of the "playmate." Every effort was made for her to seem like the girl next door who happens to enjoy disrobing to bring pleasure to six million subscribers to the magazine.

Other nude features were somewhat less antiseptic. Bare bosoms were indicated to be a necessary ingredient to a successful party, picnic, or tête-à-tête. *Playboy* became a huge financial success and spawned a host of imitators, who generally diluted the quality of models, photography, printing, and taste. Magazine kiosks seemed to burst with magazines offering photographs of naked women of every conceivable size and shape. The capacity of males to be fascinated by female nudity was presumed insatiable.

The entrance of *Playboy* into the magazine industry caused a major upheaval. In showing nudes and becoming a financial success, *Playboy* entered a field that had previously been the province of cheap "nature" and "girlie" magazines. Many of these magazines, in order to survive, moved toward the more lurid, sensational, bizarre, and pornographic. Certainly new magazines were started to appeal to those bored with mere nudity.

After *Playboy,* cheesecake became tame. Even respectable family-type magazines felt the urge to run at least occasional nude photographs and to publish articles on the "sexual revolution." At the very least they did cover articles on the *"playboy* phenomenon." The bizarre, the occult, in whatever endeavor, be it religion, politics, or sex, became important subjects to serious magazines.

One sidelight to this brief chronicle of changing attitudes toward sex needs to be mentioned. The plethora of descriptions of ecstatic sex and photographs of bosomy women simply did not fit into the human experience. A whole new field of publishing and even a new industry developed as a result.

Large numbers of Americans who had previously thought their sex lives to be fulfilling were puzzled because they did not have the ecstatic, earthmoving experiences of the characters in books. Many people attempting extramarital sex found difficulty in abandoning thoughts of guilt and tawdriness. It was not like the books. Similar problems resulted from the nude photos. Most females found their figures compared unfavorably with those in the photos and some became disturbed. Males also became disturbed because they could not seem to find and date females who looked like the photographs.

One of the results of all this was a widespread determination by large numbers of people that there was something wrong with them sexually. The publishing industry reacted with a veritable tide of "sex manuals," "how to," and "advice" books, articles, and newspaper columns. Doctors and psychologists became authors. All offered detailed information and instructions on how to improve the reader's sex life. Important scientific inquiries were begun to learn still more about the process.

Concerns about the figure spawned a new industry. The nation went diet crazy, with millions of people struggling with the knife, fork, and calorie counter to attain or retain a lithe, nubile figure. Manufacturers hastened to develop and market a host of mechanical gadgets, creams, lotions, or whatever to built the bust, reduce the waist or hips, or otherwise improve the figure wrought by nature. Cosmetics and fashions were developed to mask what could not be changed. If all else failed, doctors stood by with plastic injections or other operations to cope with hopeless cases.

One can only imagine the reactions of Anthony Comstock were he to pay a short visit to the nineteen-seventies.

It is obvious from this brief review of the publishing activities that public tastes have changed. Worries over the "impure" have given way to concerns over the orgiastic. The question is, What caused it? Did public attitudes change and cause the publishing industry to keep pace? Or did that which was published influence public attitudes? Or both? This is perhaps a chicken-or-egg-which-came-first question, but it is worthy of discussion.

It is unthinkable that Hemingway, in writing *For Whom the Bell Tolls,* considered whether a love scene between Jordan and Maria was what the public wanted to read. He wrote it because it advanced his story, expanded his characters, heightened the commentary he was making on life as he saw it, or served some other artistic purpose. It is likewise unthinkable that Hemingway set out to write a deliberately erotic scene that would set the cash registers jingling.

Can the same be said for all writers? It is a brave person who seeks to ascribe motives to writers, but some reviewers do it routinely, and more than a few authors have taken umbrage at suggestions that they are motivated by a desire to make money or demean their talent by pandering to public appetites for salacious material. Among them is Irving Wallace, author of *The Chapman Report, The Prize, The Word,* and other novels containing a generous amount of copulation. He had been listed as a "problem author" in an article in the *Library Jour-*

*nal* because of his "intentionally sensational writing" that was "exploiting sensation."

Wallace replied in an article in the same publication that he had told a group of librarians that ". . . I had tried to write well, and wanted to write well, and would never cease trying to do this. It has surprised them that I did not manufacture best-sellers deliberately ('ah, let me see, let's bake it with two rapes, four adulteries, one perversion, three four-letter words') but wrote what I observed, felt and believed within my limitations." Further on in the article Wallace added this statement:

> What I resent is the slyness of some librarians, and the reviewers to whom they pay lip service, who go beyond their rightful tasks in order to impugn the motives and intentions of an author. And what concerns me, also, is that so many books are judged not for what they say, or have to say, but because their central theme troubles the reviewer or librarian, rubs his or her neuroses the wrong way, or makes his life uneasy when he or she simply wants it easy—smooth, slick and easy.

It may pose some strain for credulity to state that *all* writers have Wallace's devotion to his craft and are not pandering to sensation just a little, but let us leave literary motives out as an issue.

It seems that writers and editors and publishers, whether in books or magazines, have more influence over public opinion than they are influenced by it. They have information, viewpoints, and ideas not generally known to the public. And they have the talent to communicate that information and those ideas in an artistic manner. The very nature of their tasks requires that they remain somewhat ahead of public knowledge and thinking to report or develop that which is new, novel, stimulating, dangerous, controversial, or whatever.

Yet, it must be said that those who wrote and are writing about sex, the more salacious the better, are finding a ready audience. People bought and are buying books containing many erotic scenes, books dealing exclusively with sex, and magazines filled to the staples with epidermal photographs. People want to read about sex and know about it and think about it, and the publishing industry is providing only what people want. Besides, sex is an important part of life. It deserves a lot of coverage—no pun intended.

We have arrived at the chicken and the egg. Did public appetites for sexual material stem from so much being written about it or does this material only reflect public interest?

Although it is a matter for individual consideration, it is possible to put forth an opinion on the subject. Sex is a part of life, an important part, and being interested in it or concerned or curious about it is as natural as drawing breath. But interest in sex was heightened in the United States by the long years of censorship and Victorian-type morality that suppressed information, discussion, and healthy attitudes about the subject.

A lot of courageous writers and publishers helped to destroy this suppression by bringing sex out into the open as a part of life that can certainly explain man, if not always ennoble him.

But a lot of other writers and publishers pandered to the interest in sex that was just awakening from suppression to exploit it for profit. It does not matter whether they did it deliberately or as an exercise in intellectual dishonesty. The effect was to increase greatly public absorption in these matters. Consider one illustration. A significant number of books dealt salaciously with a relatively uncommon phenomenon, in the nineteen-forties and fifties—precocious sex among teenage girls. It is at least arguable that writers, by making the unusual seem commonplace, encouraged attitudes that such behavior was the norm and should be emulated.

Little contribution is made to any of the arts or to public attitudes about sex or to healthy sexual relations by exploitation of phony sex. By phoniness is meant tales of incredibly proportioned women with unbelievably licentious attitudes being clutched by males capable of monumental sexual heroics. By phony sex is also meant a month after month, year after year parade of air-brushed, mammarian photographs suggesting that the nice sweet girl next door runs around disrobed for public inspection. It will be a measure of our sexual maturity when such farfetched fantasies as these are greeted with a resounding chorus of guffaws.

# CHAPTER 5
## Censorship of the Movies

THE freest art form in the United States in terms of portrayal of sex is the movies. The subjects it treats and the explicit manner in which they are presented surpass even painting or the theater, traditionally the least censored of the visual art forms.

In his book *Censorship of the Movies,* Richard S. Randall wrote:

> . . . it can almost be said that anything censored as late as the early 1960s would be licensed today, and that almost anything censored today would not even have been produced for public exhibition as late as the early sixties.

It should be added that in the four years since Randall's book was published in 1968 there has occurred an almost total disappearance of movie censorship and a corresponding elevation of sexual content.

Such statements are only astounding, for movies were historically subjected to greater censorship than any other print or visual medium. They were subject to pre- or prior censorship, and may still be so censored under the law. This means the movies had to be censored and licensed before being shown to the public. Criminal penalties could be imposed for failure to do so. Such prior censorship has never been legally imposed on newspapers, magazines, books, or the theater. Censorship was invoked only after the works were published or performed.

A host of legislative bodies, backed by the Supreme Court, determined that precensorship was necessary because of the tremendous effect movies can have on an audience. The viewer sits in a darkened theater, free from outside distractions. He witnesses men and women on the screen who are life-size and frequently larger, usually presented in "living color." They move and they speak. Music enhances the dramatic effect. If the movie is good, the actors talented, and the direction astute, the viewer can become totally absorbed in the action on the screen. He is not only a viewer, but often a participant in what is taking place. At the very least he becomes emotionally involved with the characters. Laughter and tears are common audience reactions to movies. Upon leaving the theater, many movie-goers experience a "jolt" when faced with the real world outside. It is not uncommon for particularly appealing movies to remain in the viewer's memory for years, resulting in an emotional reaction each time the movie comes to mind.

The popularity of movies was a justification for censorship. A book might be extremely lewd, but it was unlikely that any child or most immature teenagers would read it. Movies were something else. Particularly after sound was introduced in 1926, virtually no reading was required. The youngest child could go to a movie, and did. Movie-going was popular among young, dating couples. Many teenagers saw several movies a week in the nineteen-thirties and forties. Films were an important medium of family entertainment. Because of the emotional impact of movies and the fact that children saw them demands for censorship were made.

Movies were also not subject to the internal restraints of

newspapers, magazines, and radio. In these media, advertisers act as censors. They are unwilling to pay money to have their products associated with material that they believe might offend the sensibilities of potential customers. Dependent upon advertising for economic survival, newspapers, magazines, and radio edit their content so as not to offend advertisers or the public. No such restraint exists in the movies, books, painting, or the theater.

Movie producers were thus quite free to film whatever they wanted. Almost immediately, long before sound, color, and other modern techniques, movie producers discovered that nudity, sex, violence, and immorality were "good box-office."

They just as quickly discovered censorship. The city of Chicago passed an ordinance in 1907 authorizing the police to prescreen all movies to be shown in the city to determine if they were suitable. New York set up a review board in 1909, the state of Pennsylvania in 1911, and Ohio and Kansas in 1913.

This form of prior censorship was challenged in the Ohio courts in 1915. It was argued that no other form of mass communication was subject to precensorship, so movies should not be either. The Supreme Court, in *Mutual Film Corporation v. Ohio,* ruled that the First Amendment did not apply to movies. They were termed "a business pure and simple, originated and conducted for profit, like other spectacles, not to be regarded . . . as part of the press of the country or as organs of public opinion." In the years that followed, nearly all states and many cities established movie censorship boards. They were empowered to delete offending passages or to refuse to license movies altogether.

But state and local censorship was unable to still the public clamor over movies in the nineteen-twenties. There was too much sex and violence. Language was offensive to some people. Various racial, ethnic, religious, and other groups objected to methods of portraying them or their ideas. The more relaxed legal definitions of obscenity being applied to books were simply not equal to the level of movie censorship de-manded by vocal elements of the public.

The movie industry sought to fend off the demands for greater movie censorship by engaging in self-regulation. Dur-ing the nineteen-twenties, the Motion Picture Producers and Distributors of America (MPPDA) was formed. Later its name was shortened to the Motion Picture Association of America (MPAA), which will be used here. Will Hays, a former postmaster general, was hired as its head and charged with preventing censorship and improving industry public re-lations.

A resolution was passed discouraging the use of contro-versial books and plays as movie subjects. Then, in 1927, a list of "don'ts" and "be carefuls" was adopted to guide pro-ducers, directors, and actors. But all were voluntary and more ignored than observed. Criticism and demand for tougher cen-sorship laws was widespread.

In 1930, the MPAA asked Martin Quigley, Sr., a Catho-lic layman and trade publisher, and the Reverend Daniel Lord, a Jesuit priest, to draft a code to guide movie produc-ers. Known as the Production Code or "Hays Code," it was a model of self-regulation at the time. But it was again volun-tary. No enforcement was provided. The cries for greater cen-sorship continued unabated.

In 1933, the National Legion of Decency was founded by the Catholic church. It began to review and rate movies for their moral content and suitability for various audiences. Its "A-1" classification designated movies considered unobjec-tionable for general patronage. "A-2" movies were morally unobjectionable for adults and adolescents. "A-3" were unobjectionable for adults. A "B" movie was morally objec-tionable in part for all, and a "C" movie was condemned.

These ratings were done with great care and they were supported by the bishops and priests and widely publicized in the Catholic press. Even Protestants and Jews made use of them as guides to movie-going. Almost immediately, the B and C ratings of the Legion of Decency came to be fatal for a movie. These films were not shown at all in predominantly Catholic neighborhoods and large numbers of non-Catholic distributors were afraid to show them. Attendance at poorly rated movies declined sharply.

Faced with effective censorship from the Catholic church, movie producers moved to make their own code more effective. A production office was set up under Hays. It was empowered to review all scripts and advise on unacceptable elements in them. When the films were finished, they were reviewed by the Hays office. Those found acceptable by conforming to the Production Code were given a seal of approval.

The agreement behind this new system was that only movies bearing the special seal would be shown in theaters owned by the members of the MPAA. These were the major film production companies, for they owned 70 percent of the operating theaters. An independent producer who sought to release a film without the seal was tempting bankruptcy.

Hays and his successors were vigorous in enforcing the code. Changes in scripts, language, camera angles, and other aspects of production were freely ordered or negotiated. Movies, already censored by the government and rated by the Legion of Decency (which rarely condemned a movie bearing the seal), now came under stiff self-regulation. Movies may not have become as pure as was hoped, but demands for further censorship largely ceased, and Hollywood embarked on its fantastic golden age of the nineteen-thirties and forties.

What was the code? All forms of nudity were banned. Nothing more revealing than a bathing suit, sweater, or negligee were permitted. Décolleté was conservative, to say the least. Nothing even remotely sensuous, let alone lewd or lascivious, was permitted. Sexual activity consisted of a kiss and that was restricted as to form and duration. Even supposedly married couples could not be shown in bed together, and premarital or extramarital sex was hardly even suggested, let alone condoned.

Violence was limited to fistfights and wrestling brawls.

Displays of blood or gore were heavily restricted. Even in western and gangster films, weapons were not to be excessively displayed or used.

All foul language was forbidden. No form of blasphemy was permitted and all forms of swear words, including the mild "hell" and "damn" were censored. The stronger four-letter words were not even considered. Such subjects as abortion were not to be mentioned at all, and special care had to be used in dealing with such matters as mercy killing, kidnapping, adultery, the clergy, and childbirth. "Double entendre" words like "fairy" or "goose" were to be avoided or used with great care.

Other provisions required that the basic dignity of human life be respected; that evil, sin, and crime not be justified, let alone go unpunished; that religion not be demeaned; that words or symbols offensive to racial, religious, or national groups not be used; that there be no excessive cruelty to animals.

The code provisions were vigorously and successfully enforced by the Hays office. Hollywood made hundreds of movies a year during the nineteen-thirties and forties. Theaters were packed. Fantastic profits were made and tremendous sums of money spent on lavish productions. Extravagantly paid actors and actresses, known as "stars," became famous, as familiar to millions of Americans as members of their own families.

The censorship issue may have largely disappeared, but another sort of criticism began to be made. First, the artistically inclined, then critics, and finally large numbers of movie-goers began to complain that Hollywood movies insulted adult intelligence. The movies presented an unreal world, a fantasy land, full of gloss and happy endings, but signifying nothing. With precious few exceptions, movies lacked realism, genuine emotion, and intellectual content. As dramatic art they were sophomoric.

More importantly, perhaps, criticisms were made that Hollywood films presented a fraudulent image of America to the rest of the world. Surveys showed that significant numbers of foreigners believed that the United States was heavily populated by cowboys and Indians or overrun by bandits and gangsters. Other impressions were that Americans were incredibly rich, living in penthouses, expensively dressed in tuxedos and fur coats, and much given to attending nightclubs and musical extravaganzas. All women were virtuous, men were hard-working or hen-pecked, blacks were empty-headed and incurably happy-go-lucky, and children were invariably cute, mischievous, and foolish.

It became rather apparent that Hollywood, clamped under a reign of externally and internally imposed censorship—although few blamed censorship for the decline in the quality of films—was wasting a medium with a high potential for artistic, social, political, and intellectual communication.

Hollywood fell on dark economic days in the late nineteen-forties and early nineteen-fifties. Attendance at theaters dropped 50 percent; profits dwindled; the number of movies produced declined sharply; studios closed; movie personnel, both famous and unknown, went unemployed. The golden age of Hollywood was over.

Much of this decline was blamed on the rise of television. People could see old movies and be entertained in their homes. Why go to the theater? Television was undoubtedly significant, but the widespread boredom and dissatisfaction with the movies Hollywood was making was also a factor. Foreign movies, notably those from Italy, Sweden, France, England, and Japan, began to be widely distributed in the United States. They offered a high degree of realism, dramatic impact, and social importance. Hollywood's products suffered by comparison. Clearly censorship, even if self-imposed, was a two-edge sword that cut a wide swath through the motion picture industry.

The self-regulation imposed by the Production Code began to be loosened. A serious blow was dealt in 1948 when the Supreme Court, in an antitrust action, ordered the major Hollywood studios to divest themselves of the theaters they owned. This undermined the method of enforcing the Production Code. Theaters owned by the major studios would not show any movie that did not bear the special seal of approval. With the theaters now independent of the studios, they were free to show the movies they wished, seal or no seal. The door was opened for the more controversial and erotic foreign films, and they entered.

The Production Code lingered on. Under the chafing of producers and directors, it was revised. In 1956, the taboos against narcotics, prostitution, and miscegenation (interracial marriage) were lifted. In 1961, it was further amended to allow homosexuality and other sexual aberrations to be film subjects if "treated with care, discretion and restraint." Controversial films were to bear the label "suggested for mature audiences" even though no effort was made to define what constituted a "mature audience."

The chief effect of the new code was to give the Production Code Administration considerable discretion in deciding on the acceptability of content. The across-the-board bans on such content as nudity, brutality, and profanity were liberalized. Thus, a brief nude scene was permitted in *The Pawnbroker* and much profanity was allowed in *Who's Afraid of Virginia Woolf?* This was viewed as a distinct improvement from the days not long before when the entire motivation of characters in *Tea and Sympathy* and *Cat on a Hot Tin Roof,* both adapted from the theater, had to be changed because of the ban on homosexuality as a theme.

Significant is the fact that *The Pawnbroker* and *Virginia Woolf,* while both considered among the finer films of their times, were produced in the mid-nineteen-sixties. Hollywood was decades behind books, magazines, and the theater in its treatment of sexual themes, and it wanted to catch up. An industry spokesman said the old code, drafted in the nineteen-thirties "reflected the mores of a depression and puritanical era." It was now "unrealistic" and "neither reflected nor conformed to the mores of a contemporary society." Cited as evidence were stories of "wife swapping and campus cohabitation" in newspapers, discussions of birth control, adultery, and abortion in women's magazines, "full-page spreads of nudes" in magazines.

A new code was released in 1966 that sought to conform to "contemporary standards as they are portrayed in other media." Although it was much briefer and far more liberal, it was still high-minded.

> Evil, sin, crime, and wrong-doing shall not be justified; detailed and protracted acts of brutality, cruelty, physical violence, torture and abuse shall not be presented; indecent or undue exposure of the human body shall not be presented; intimate sex scenes violating common standards of decency shall not be portrayed; restraint and care shall be exercised in presentations dealing with sex aberrations; obscene speech, gestures or movements shall not be presented; undue profanity shall not be permitted; religion shall not be demeaned.

But it was not to be for long. The code made censorship difficult. A variety of interpretations could be placed on such words as *detailed* and *protracted, indecent* and *undue, common standards, restraint* and *care,* and, of course, *obscene.*

Two other factors played significant roles in undermining censorship of the movies. The first was the courts. The first major decision came in 1952 and involved the Italian film, *The Miracle,* directed by Roberto Rossellini and starring Anna Magnani. It was a tale of an unmarried, Italian peasant woman who became pregnant by a passing vagrant. She believed Saint Joseph had caused her to conceive. She was taunted in the village and endured ordeals at the birth of her child.

The film opened in an "art" theater in New York. Shortly thereafter, New York City's commissioner of licenses banned it as "officially and personally blasphemous." The Legion of Decency condemned it and leading clerics, such as Francis Cardinal Spellman, archbishop of New York, denounced it. Censors of the state of New York also banned the movie. Joseph Burstyn, the distributor of the film, took the issue to the courts. It reached the Supreme Court in 1952, and Burstyn and the movie won. The court ruled that movies enjoyed the protection of the First Amendment, along with newspapers and magazines. The justices also decided that ". . . a state may not ban a film on the basis of a censor's conclusion that it is sacrilegious." The term "sacrilegious" was declared to be too imprecise to permit standards for determining what was or was not filmable. In later years, the court termed such words as "immoral" or "harmful" or "sexual immorality" as too imprecise as guidelines for movie producers.

In the wake of *The Miracle* and companion decisions, Ohio courts declared its movie censorship law illegal. Pennsylvania judges declared censorship unconstitutional. In state after state movie censorship was either declared illegal or abandoned as a waste of time and tax money. By 1970, only Maryland continued to go through the rather ritualistic exercise of attempting to precensor films.

This abandonment of prior censorship, however, was passing, for in 1961, the Supreme Court ruled in *Times Film Corporation v. Chicago* that precensorship of movies was legal in America. The issue was brought before the court deliberately. Chicago required that before a movie could be shown in that city, it had to be submitted to the commissioner of police for censorship. The Times Film Corporation refused to submit a movie entitled *Don Juan*. Based on Mozart's opera, it was hardly obscene by any standards. When the issue reached the Supreme Court, the justices decided in a five to four vote that prior censorship was justified. Justice Tom Clark, in his majority opinion, argued that communities could not be stripped of "all constitutional power to prevent, in the most effective fashion, what might possibly offend the community."

The decision earned a long and blistering dissent from Chief Justice Earl Warren. He spoke of the "real danger" the majority decision offered for "eventual censorship for every form of communication, be it newspapers, journals, books, magazines, television, radio or public speeches. . . ." He castigated the majority for permitting one medium, motion pictures, to be subjected to prior censorship, while other media were immune. He referred to the "evils" and "mischief" of the censor, saying it "impedes all communication by hanging threateningly over creative thought."

The chief justice listed some of the films that had been victims of censorship in various communities: a scene showing the birth of a buffalo in Walt Disney's *Vanishing Prairie; Curley* because it showed black and white children playing together; the words "Oh, God, why has thou forsaken me?" as uttered by the saint in *Joan of Arc; Anatomy of a Murder* because it used the words "rape" and "contraceptive"; *Professor Mamlock,* which showed the persecution of Jews in Nazi Germany, on the grounds it was "communistic propaganda"; *The Southerner* because its depiction of poverty among tenant farmers "reflects on the South."

Some writers on censorship have tended to deplore the court's decision in the Times Film Corporation case as a setback for free expression and evidence of discrimination against the motion picture industry. Author Richard S. Randall points out in *Censorship of the Movies* that the decision lessened rather than heightened censorship. The number of censorship boards declined following the decision. Judges tended to cite the Warren dissent rather than the majority opinion in striking down censorship—or to ignore the majority ruling.

In 1965, the Supreme Court all but declared prior censorship illegal. It said such censorship could occur, but declared that procedural safeguards must be provided, such as prompt judicial review of the censor's decision. This made the work of the censorship boards far more difficult.

Various state and federal appellate courts ruled not obscene movies containing sex between a sixteen-year-old boy and a woman old enough to be his mother; nude sex scenes between two unmarried people; sex between a married woman and her paramour; nude embraces between two lesbians in a girls' school; a Swedish film that depicted sodomy, intercourse with a prostitute, a homosexual act, and self-mutilation.

The court's opinion in the latter movie was typical of the reasoning in many of the other cases. The court declared the movie "repulsive, revolting and disgusting," but added:

> . . . but to attribute to this two-hour picture, attempting to deal with social problems which in 1966 are not only on our doorstep but very much over the threshold, such a purpose is completely to misunderstand and misview the picture and its message.

That such movies were made and distributed in respectable theaters is the second reason for the undermining of Hollywood's Production Code. A number of producers and directors discovered they could violate the Production Code, show movies without the seal of approval, and make fortunes.

Four major types of films flaunted both the letter and the spirit of the code. *Exploitation* films, as they are called in the industry, seek "shock or salacity," as Randall put it. Examples are nudist camp films, "nudie" films of the burlesque variety with generous displays of breasts and buttocks, movies dealing with provocative subjects such as abortion, perversion, wife-swapping, drug addiction, wayward girls, vice dens of Europe, etc., and those films portraying sadism and masochism. Some dip close to the "stag film" level, while others at least maintain a pretense of the documentary approach. All are made inexpensively.

The exploitation film has long been produced, but until the last few years it was a "back door" enterprise. Little pride was taken in the work. Those involved were hardly likely to brag about their accomplishment. Only the seediest, lowest-class theaters ran them. Then in 1959, the movie *The Immoral Mr. Teas* was released. It was built around a single joke, a man who had a talent (or perhaps affliction) for seeing clothed women in a state of undress. Made for only $24,000, it grossed over $1 million and ran for over two years in Hollywood.

Such a financial success led others to enter the business, either to make films or to purchase and distribute foreign-made exploitation films. Their quality improved. Hundreds of better theaters, even first-rate houses, began to offer such films on a more or less regular basis.

*Art* films, the second type, also began to flourish under the lagging enforcement of censorship. These are high-quality films with excellent scripts, photography, acting, and direction. They seek to innovate and develop motion pictures as a means of artistic expression. They explore controversial themes that never would have passed the censors just a few years ago. They depend, like the theater, on reviews in newspapers and magazines and play largely in small art theaters. Many are foreign films, such as the Italian *L'Avventura* and *8½*; the Swedish films of Ingmar Bergman; the French *Hiroshima, Mon Amour* and *La Guerre Est Finie;* Japan's *Woman in the Dunes* and *Rashomon;* the Irish *Ulysses;* the British *Saturday Night and Sunday Morning* and *A Taste of Honey.* American examples were *David and Lisa, One Potato, Two Potato,* and *The Pawnbroker.*

*Experimental* films begin where art films end. Often done by amateurs and sometimes called "underground" films, they deal with experimentation in lighting, sound, action, acting, and film editing. Again, by their very nature they deal many times with sexual and sensational subjects. The most famous maker of such films is the American Andy Warhol.

Faced with the financial success and growing respectability of the exploitation films and the critical success of the art films, the makers of *major* films sought to keep pace. Major films are expensive productions made in large studios with name actors and directors. They are extravagantly promoted and run in the first-line theaters. These too went the way of flesh, purchasing sex-laden best sellers and translating them to the screen. Examples include *Lolita, Fanny Hill, Tropic of Cancer, Candy, Valley of the Dolls,* and *The Carpetbaggers.* By the very nature of these books, the films had to depict such acts as rape, abortion, and wholesale violence. Accompanying the mayhem was a new "realism," spurting blood, gaping wounds, and appropriate screams and groans. Nudity, sensual caresses, and explicit sex became the rule.

Thus, the Production Code was reduced to a glittering generality, and movie theaters came to offer, if only vicariously, the fare formerly reserved for whore houses and hospital emergency rooms. Hollywood may have come full circle, but it was still questionable whether it offered any more genuine and realistic representation of American life than it had back in the heyday of the Hays office in the nineteen-forties.

A predictable result of the new, liberalized films was a clamor for censorship. The label "suggested for mature audiences" was hardly able to keep large numbers of adults from being offended, revolted, or disgusted by the Hollywood products or parents from being horrified that their children might see the films.

What could be done? Legal censorship of movies was virtually dead. Little was attempted and the courts regularly struck down that which was accomplished. Private organizations such as the Legion for Decency, now called the National Catholic Office for Motion Pictures, continued to review and rate pictures. Another famous rating was the "green sheet" put out by the Film Board of National Organizations, an amalgam of ten national organizations concerned about film fare.*

Other private ratings were made by *Parents Magazine, Consumer Report,* the *Parent-Teachers Association Magazine, Consumer Bulletin,* the *Protestant Motion Picture Bulletin,* the *Daughters of the American Revolution Magazine,* and the *Christian Science Monitor.*

All these efforts were intended to alert citizens, particu-

---

* The American Jewish Committee, the American Library Association, the Daughters of the American Revolution, the Federation of Motion Picture Council, the General Federation of Women's Clubs, the National Congress of Parents and Teachers, the National Council of Women of the United States of America, the National Federation of Music Clubs, the Protestant Motion Picture Council, and the School Motion Picture Committee.

larly parents, to the subject and content of new movies. The aim was to have censorship occur in the home with individuals deciding what they did not want to see or want their children to see.

These national efforts, most undertaken by professional censors and experts in art, psychology, and child development, were augmented by a host of more informal community activities. Clergymen spoke out against certain films from their pulpits. Women's, fraternal, service, and veterans' organizations spread the word among members. Neighborhood parents circulated "reviews," usually condemnatory, among themselves. Motion picture producers were beseiged by mail. Theater managers who showed objectionable films were badgered, threatened, and picketed. Some violence even occurred.

All the efforts were something less than wholly successful. Film producers were able to point out that the number of "wholesome" films made equaled or surpassed that of exploitive ones. Theater managers showed attendance figures that proved that the "dirty" movies played to packed houses while the nonobjectionable ones lost money. They often asked objecting parents if they had seen the wholesome movie that played last week. Many had not. The managers suggested they had to show the films the audiences wanted to see, which meant those containing sex and violence.

Informal or voluntary censorship also failed because many, perhaps most, parents were too unconcerned to investigate the movies their children were seeing. It was too easy simply to drop the children off at the theater, paying no mind to what they saw. Other parents simply did not care and not a few did not believe any movies were harmful.

Opponents of censorship joined the fray, attacking any form of censorship, and portraying those who actively fought the showing of certain films as prudes.

The ruckus was heard in Hollywood, if only in terms of declining theater attendance and profits. The industry yearned for its golden days, and sought ways to recapture public respect for its sense of responsibility.

After years of resisting suggestions that it classify its films for subject matter and audience appeal, the industry did an about face and accepted classification in November 1968.

In announcing the new system, Jack Valenti, president of the MPAA, said movie makers should have as much freedom as "those who write books, produce television material, publish newspapers and magazines, compose music and create paintings and sculpture." But that freedom should be responsible, he said, and added:

There are many audiences and if we seek out the lowest common audience denominator, we will find ourselves making movies that would be . . . inane. We cannot allow children to set the boundaries for motion picture creativity, any more than we would allow children to organize our moral apparatus or our national priorities. But we can be concerned about children.

So, a rating system was announced that was concerned about children. All movies would be rated according to audience appeal. As later revised, the ratings are:

> G—All ages admitted.
> PG—All ages admitted, but parental guidance recommended.
> R—Anyone under seventeen must be accompanied by a parent or legal guardian.
> X—No one under eighteen admitted.

The rating of every picture was to be prominently displayed in the theater and in the advertising for the film. Theater managers were charged with policing the theater to see that children were not admitted to inappropriate pictures.

After some confusion, the rating system began to work effectively. Parental complaints subsided. Hollywood's reputation for responsibility improved.

The ratings make no attempt at censorship. Producers are

free to make just about any movie they believe they can sell. If anything, films became more daring. All the ratings do is warn parents about the picture.

It had originally been thought that an "X" rating would be the kiss of death for a movie. But not so. Attendance soared at many of them, the X being the best advertisement that the film was full of sex and violence, or at least controversy. Films that were rated X even won academy awards for "best picture of the year," notably "Midnight Cowboy" in 1969.

Thus, Hollywood did not solve the censorship problem any more than book or magazine publishers did. The movie industry simply avoided it with a rating system that removed the principal objection of the public, that there were films children should not see. There are those who consider that a debatable point, but at least adults wanting to see controversial or salacious movies are not prevented from doing so.

# CHAPTER 6
# Censorship of Television

ALTHOUGH it would seem to be otherwise, television is the most heavily censored medium of communication in America today. There is no great uproar about obscenity on the tube. Nothing resembling the movie rating system exists. Criticisms are voiced, particularly about the amount of violence shown, but there are few if any citizens groups spreading the word about what shows children should not watch.

But the lack of censorship activity aimed at television is the result of the highly effective censorship that occurs before a show ever reaches the air.

The censorship comes from four main sources. First, advertisers play an important role in screening out the offensive. With the exception of the public broadcasting stations and educational television, all television in America is commercially supported. Even those few programs that are not sponsored are supported by the networks or individual stations from profits made on sponsored programs.

Business and industry may sponsor entire programs, underwriting the cost of producing the show and the cost of the air time. They may share such costs with other companies by buying only a part of a show or by sponsoring it biweekly or monthly. Perhaps the most popular method of advertising is through "spot" commercials in or between regular programming. Possibly one-quarter of television time is devoted to advertising.

It is extremely costly to advertise on television. A half-hour network show may cost well over $150,000 a week. Millions of dollars may be spent on advertising a single product on television. Obviously, only large firms marketing products or services that will have mass appeal can afford such costs.

It is axiomatic that no advertiser will spend such sums on any program that he believes will be offensive to the public. Because he is trying to reach large numbers of existing and potential customers with his "message," he cannot run the risk of being identified with any program that is in bad taste, let alone possibly obscene. In all but rare instances, the advertiser does not want to be identified with even controversial programs and protects himself with such announcements as "The views expressed on this program are entirely those of Mr. So and So and do not necessarily reflect those of this station, the network, or the XYZ Company."

Thus, television networks and individual stations, working very hard to attract advertisers, try to offer programs that have little or no possibility of offending anyone. Advertisers, because of their large investment, frequently are able to censor programs. At the very least, the tacit knowledge that programs will be canceled if no advertiser wants them leads producers and directors to avoid offensive or controversial material.

Second, the commercial networks perform censorship. Most television stations belong to either the American Broadcasting Company (ABC), the Columbia Broadcasting System (CBS) or the National Broadcasting Company (NBC). These are profit-making organizations. They produce and sell nationwide programs as well as air time and advertising. They are in direct competition with one another for the attention of the viewing audience. National surveys are made in the hopes of determining what percentage of the viewers is watching which network's show at any given time. The popularity of the network and its individual programs are used to attract advertisers.

Thus each network has a large financial stake in the quality of its programming. It rigidly controls the programs it transmits to its member stations. It tries to avoid offending advertisers, member stations that might refuse to carry a specific program, or the viewing public, which can always turn to another channel or shut off the set. The networks most definitely perform a powerful censorship function. They can decide which programs to televise; they can precensor existing programs, as CBS did some years ago with the "Smothers Brothers Comedy Hour"; they can snip out individual words, as NBC did not long ago, editing out the word "peace" as uttered on Johnny Carson's "Tonight Show."

Third, the industry engages in self-regulation. All networks and individual stations subscribe to a national television code listing do's and don't's for producers and advertisers. It is amazingly similar to the old Hollywood code—no nudity, sex, undue violence, profanity, blasphemy, or cruelty to animals is allowed. Crime must not pay, lawlessness or antisocial conduct may not be justified, minority groups may not be offended.

Unlike Hollywood, which did not have the problem, the Television Code has guidelines for advertisers. No hard liquor may be advertised. Beer and wine may be advertised, as long as no one is shown drinking to excess, enjoying it too much, or acting as though he were in a typical bar. At the most the model may bring the brew to his lips, but not taste it. There are prohibitions against ads for cigarettes, contraceptive devices, personal hygiene products, and many medicines, such as those for hemorrhoids. Ads for other products, such as those for toilet tissue or deodorants, may be used, if done in "good taste."

The code was prepared in 1952 by the National Association of Broadcasters, which has a similar code for radio. The NAB operates a Code Authority in Washington headed by Stockton Helffrich, who has described himself as a "reluctant censor." In an article in the August 23, 1969 issue of *TV Guide*, Mr. Helffrich saw his job as keeping television abreast of the times without offending viewers, which qualifies as a difficult feat.

He said society is "tolerating great candor" which the television industry tries to keep up with. "Young people today, for instance, are more honest and candid in their approach to sex," he said. He did not specify how it was possible to be candid without offending, except to say the networks were responding "to a greater openness on the part of the audience, while not pressing it too far."

That was certainly open to a variety of interpretations. In 1971, Senator John Pastore of Rhode Island, who has taken a particular interest in "sex and violence" on television, said the industry code lacked enforcement and called upon broadcasters to "clean up the dirt" on television.

Senator Pastore was perhaps reacting to reports of the National Commission on Violence that the "constant portrayal of violence" on television was "pandering to a public preoccupation with violence that television itself has helped to create." The commission has said that "violence on television encourages violent forms of behavior and fosters moral and social values about violence in daily life which are unacceptable in a civilized society." The commission deplored the fact that ". . . we daily permit our children during their formative years to enter a world of police interrogations, of gangsters beating enemies, of spies performing fatal brain surgery and of routine demonstration of all kinds of killing and maiming."

As a result of these and other public criticisms, the National Association of Broadcasters empowered Mr. Helffrich's office to begin precensoring television shows for sex and violence. Television spokesmen have stated that they believe the prior censorship has alleviated the problem.

The fourth and most potent censorship force on television

is the federal government. There are only a limited number of broadcasting channels, and these are parceled out to stations licensed by the Federal Communications Commission (FCC). Congress specifically forbade the FCC from censoring broadcasting, but it did authorize the agency to see that broadcasting stations operate in the public interest. Station licenses are granted only to financially responsible individuals and companies and for only a stated period of years. Historically, the licenses are renewed automatically, but the FCC clearly has the power to revoke a license from a station that does not operate in the public interest.

As a result, radio and television stations routinely broadcast "public service" announcements and programs on behalf of government, religious, or other groups. Examples would be programs on behalf of enlistment in the military services, safe driving warnings, appeals for church going, fire safety, book reading, cooperation with the police, joining the Red Cross, and similar activities. At the license renewal time, stations are able to show how many hours of broadcasting time were devoted to "public service."

The legal processes are a bit murky, but it is certainly feared that the FCC could refuse to renew licenses for those stations it believed engaged in programming of sex, violence, or whatever were not in the "public interest." The mere threat of trouble over relicensing is enough to keep television programs clean.

An example of the power of the FCC was the statement in March 1972, by Dean Burch, FCC chairman, castigating the television industry for "needless and gratuitous violence" in children's programming. Addressing a Senate subcommittee, Mr. Burch urged advertisers to "exercise leadership and leverage" on behalf of better programming. He called upon the industry to make a "good faith effort" to "capitalize on the affirmative capabilities of television to enrich the experience of young viewers." He said he would dislike to use the FCC's licensing power to this purpose, but he felt "joint consultation is essential" to solve the problem.

Another federal agency that is subtle but powerful is the Federal Trade Commission. After years of moribund acquiescence to "business as usual," it has begun to crack down in recent years on worthless products and fraudulent advertising. Such techniques as photographing wine instead of coffee, putting marbles in soup to hold up the vegetables so there seems to be more of them, offering worthless "guarantees" and generally misleading the public have been banned. Advertisers have been put on the defensive to prove the truth of their claims, which also means stating what products *cannot* do along with what they *can* do.

With these forces influencing it, television can rightly claim to be the most censored medium of communication in America. What is amazing is not that television sometimes does so poorly under its load of censorship, but that it sometimes does so well.

As the matter now stands, the heavy censorship of television poses some difficulties. The biggest is the often stated criticism that television is an "intellectual wasteland." There is relatively little programming that bears much potential for controversy. Most television time is devoted to sports, news and public events programs, old movies that had already been approved and had run in theaters, quiz and game shows, programs for children, music and variety shows, and reruns of old programs that had been popular and accepted the first time they were shown. Perhaps only two or three hours a day are devoted to new programs that bear much risk of rebuke.

A slave to the clock, television runs most serials in half-hour and hour segments, all regularly interrupted by commercials.* The programs are heavily oriented toward plot and action. Only the most superficial characterizations are possible. Insight, character development, and social comment are diffi-

---

* When American programs are seen on European television, they have more dramatic impact, probably because there are no interruptions for commercials. Interestingly, the "hour" show in the United States takes only forty-five minutes or so in Europe, without commercials. In Europe, commercials are run in five and ten minute segments between programs.

cult to find. Truly dramatic programs of artistic merit are rarities.

There is nothing wrong with broadcasting entertainment. The problem, according to the criticisms, is that the programs are not very entertaining. They appeal to the immature, the adolescent, and the bored. Everything is highly forgettable. Simply try to remember stimulating programs from last week, last month, or last year. Only rarely does television compare favorably with the better motion picture or theater productions. Only in broadcasting live sports, for those who are interested, does television create a distinctive form of entertainment.

The failure of television as a medium of entertainment, the sheer boredom it creates among both viewers and nonviewers, is analogous to the movies of the 1950s. Television offers a similar sort of unreal, fantasy world divorced from the cares and concerns of real people. Little is done that is original or innovative. Only rarely is dramatic material offered that enlarges the viewers' skein of experience or their understanding of life. Television can make few pretensions to being an art medium.

There may well be several causes for this, but one certainly is the depth of censorship imposed on television. Few of the better writers, novelists, playwrights, and screenwriters write for television because the taboos make it extremely difficult to write honestly and meaningfully of human experience. To give but one example, there is no way Hemingway's scene between Jordan and Maria could be shown realistically on television.

With so much forbidden or constrained, television, in its search for candor, has dug deep into the well of violence in its western and adventure stories. Unable realistically to portray human joys and fears based upon sex, or to deal honestly with such matters as divorce, sexual deviation, religion, politics, dissent, pacifism, race, even obscenity itself, television is left to sustain its demand for candor and action through violence and phony sex. New themes, new social commentaries are a study in human ingenuity for television. The half-hour and hour formats, the constant interruptions for commercials make the medium difficult at best, but the squads of censors certainly assist in making it an intellectually and artistically dead medium.

When television was first developed, many people saw its tremendous potential for informing, enlightening, and inspiring Americans. In many ways, it has fulfilled that potential in the field of news and public affairs. It made Americans virtual participants as men walked and rode on the moon. The horrors and futility of the war in Vietnam have been displayed on television screens in nearly every home in America. Citizens have seen the presidential nominating conventions and seen politicians of high and low stature both at work and campaigning. Important changes in our political system have resulted. A very long list could be cited to show the impact of television public affairs programs. Even so, extensive criticisms have been made of television news and related programs, which we will discuss in Part II.

The point being made here is that television has not lived up to its potential as a cultural medium. It offers basically light entertainment, most of which is banal. No original art form has developed from the medium. Only a relative handful of important creative works have been written for television. Little progress has been made in broadening public tastes for better literature, theater, or arts.

There are again several reasons for this, but one of them must be the effects of censorship.

# CHAPTER 7
# Should Obscenity Be Censored?

OUR excursion into the history of censorship in America has revealed some information that may be helpful in answering the cardinal question: Should we censor obscenity?

We have discovered that (1) censorship has really only been a problem for about the last century; (2) the emphasis of censorship has been mostly on sexual material, with ancillary concerns about violence, profanity, and blasphemy; (3) censorship has been a major concern of essentially private groups that have encouraged the passage of penal laws involving police action against obscenity; (4) courts have in recent decades declared most of the antiobscenity laws unconstitutional and have taken a quite narrow view of what obscenity is; (5) private censorship groups have taken effective private actions to force movies and television to impose self-regulation.

Two more conjectural hypotheses can be drawn from our look at history. The first is that the publication and depiction of sexual material may have incited public interest in these subjects. The second is that severe censorship may have adversely influenced the artistic creativity and relevancy of movies, television, and possibly printed material.

It is certainly true that a great deal of discussion is going on in the United States about obscenity and censorship. Many arguments are raised both for and against censorship. As usually presented they pose a nearly unsolvable problem, for appealing arguments are offered on both sides. It would seem that the best that rational, well-intentioned individuals can do is to agree to disagree. Perhaps. But working on the premise that no problem is entirely unsolvable, it may be possible to arrive at, if not a solution, a new way of thinking about the problems.

The arguments for and against censorship may be lumped under two broad categories: the rights of the individual versus the protection of society; and the practical difficulties of censorship.

The question of individual rights is an edge that cuts both ways. It is most commonly used as a basis of attack upon all forms of censorship. An individual in the United States is allowed to say or write nearly anything. It is a freedom guaranteed by the First Amendment to the Constitution.

The fear is that censorship of the obscene, no matter how well meant or how large the public agreement on the matter, will lead to censorship of political, religious, and other ideas entirely unrelated to obscenity. This view was expressed by the late Justice Hugo L. Black:

> It is the duty of the courts to be watchful for the constitutional rights of the citizen, and against any stealthy encroachments thereon. While it is "obscenity and indecency" before us today, the experience of mankind—both ancient and modern—shows that this type of elastic phrase can, and most likely will, be synonymous with the political, and maybe with the religious, unorthodoxy of tomorrow. Censorship is the deadly enemy of freedom and progress.

Similar views have been expressed several times by Justice William O. Douglas. One of his most eloquent expressions came in a 1966 dissent:

. . . The First Amendment allows all ideas to be expressed —whether orthodox, popular, off-beat, or repulsive. I do not think it permissible to draw lines between the "good" and the "bad" and be true to the constitutional mandate to let all ideas alone. If our Constitution permitted "reasonable" regulations of freedom of expression, as do the constitutions of some nations, we would be in a field where the legislative and the judiciary would have much leeway. But under our charter all regulation or control of expression is barred. Government does not sit to reveal where the "truth" is. People are left to pick and choose between competing offerings. There is no compulsion to take and read what is repulsive any more than there is to spend one's time pouring over government bulletins, political tracts, or theological treatises. The theory is that people are mature enough to pick and choose, to recognize trash when they see it, to be attracted to the literature that satisfies their deepest need, and hopefully, to move from plateau to plateau and finally reach the world of enduring ideas.

I think this is the ideal of the Free Society written into our Constitution. We have no business acting as censors or endowing any group with censorship powers. It is shocking to me for us to send to prison anyone for publishing anything. . . .

A more succinct statement came from the late Justice John Marshall Harlan. The government, he said,

has no business, whether under the postal or commerce power, to bar the sale of books because they might lead to any kind of "thoughts."

Justice Douglas again:

. . . the test that suppresses a cheap tract today can suppress a literary gem tomorrow. All it need do is incite a lascivious thought or arouse a lustful desire. The list of books that judges or juries can place in that category is endless.

Finally, we should ponder a statement made by Dan Lacy,

representing the American Book Publishers Council before a House Committee in 1960:

> The five countries that today probably most consistently and thoroughly, through government and industry means, apply a control over the content of publications in the area of sex are Communist China, Ireland, Russia, South Africa and Spain. It is by no means an accidental coincidence that all of these also practice an extensive political censorship of varying degree; but here I am speaking only of moral censorship and its consequences. Though such a control by no means prevents writings of moral vacuity and disorientation, it is quite successful in eliminating salacious and obscene writing and the overdramatization of sex. It has also, in the process, substantially eliminated from those countries the main body of contemporary world literature. Almost no Western novelists appear in China; few in Russia. Among world renowned authors whose writing have been banned from Ireland are Theodore Dreiser, Sherwood Anderson, James Branch Cabell, Sinclair Lewis, Aldous Huxley, William Faulkner, Lillian Smith, Erich Remarque, John Steinbeck, and James T. Farrell. . . .
>
> The consequences are seen not only in this blocking of international flow of masterpieces of contemporary world literature, but also in the drying up of creative writing within those countries. All, with the partial exception of South Africa, are countries of the richest creative tradition; but their literature lives today only in the sort of rebellion against the controlling morality expressed by an O'Casey, a Pasternak, or a Paton.

To summarize, censorship of obscene materials violates the First Amendment freedoms, may lead to censorship of political and religious ideas, and suppresses creativity in all its forms.

The reverse edge of the individual freedoms argument is as follows: a person also has a right *not* to read or have himself visually assaulted by pornography. He has the right to be protected against receiving unsolicited pornography in the mail; against having himself exposed to pornography in such public places as newsstands or sidewalks underneath movie marquees; and against having his moral training of his children undermined by their exposure to pornography.

The argument can be stated in broader terms. Sex is an intensely private matter. Individuals can reasonably object to having a private matter constantly paraded in public, even if in general terms. Women can certainly object to wholesale displays of female nudity, and their demeaning portrayal as nothing more than sexual objects.

In short, the freedom to express ideas conflicts with the freedom of a person to make his own choices of ideas he wishes to know or deems important.

This conflict is not unsolvable. The Commission on Obscenity and Pornography, which recommended the abandonment of all government censorship as unworkable, also recommended regulation of pornographic displays in public places, such as newsstands and theater marquees. Another similar suggestion came from Irving Kristol, a professor at New York University, in a *New York Times Magazine* article on March 28, 1971, entitled, "Pornography, Obscenity and the Case for Censorship." He suggested a return to the former practice of selling pornography under the counter. Those who want it can have it, but those who are revolted by it do not have to see it. Denmark, which legalized pornography, regulates displays of it before the public.

The issue of protecting society is most complex. Its central question is this: Is obscene and pornographic material harmful?

It is an article of faith among the majority of Americans that it is. This widespread public view was stated in 1959 by the late J. Edgar Hoover, long-time director of the Federal Bureau of Investigation.

What we do know is that an overwhelmingly large number of cases of sex crime is associated with pornography. We know that sex criminals read it, are clearly influenced by it. I believe pornography is a major cause of sex violence. I believe that if we can eliminate the distribution of such items among impressionable schoolage children, we shall greatly reduce our frightening crime rate.

A very long list of such opinions could be quoted.

Inspector Harry Fox, commander of the Juvenile Aid Division of the Philadelphia Police Department: "My men and I have questioned hundreds of . . . the juveniles involved, and we believe . . . that this material [pornography] acts as an aphrodisiac resulting in rapes, seductions, sodomy, indecent assaults, and indecent exposure."

Dr. Benjamin Karpman, a psychiatrist, in 1956 told the 84th Congressional Senate Subcommittee Investigating Juvenile Delinquency that pornographic material draws a young boy "into all sorts of gang life, which discharges itself as juvenile delinquency."

In 1967, before the House Select Subcommittee on Education, Dr. Nicholas Frignito, chief neuropsychiatrist of the Philadelphia Municipal Court, told of "criminal behavior from vicious assaults to homicide" that derived from "arousal from smutty books." He added:

> Some of these children did not transgress sexually until they read suggestive stories and viewed lewd pictures in licentious magazines. In several instances the children were very young, varying in age from 9 to 14 years. The filthy ideas implanted in their immature minds impelled them to crime.

Perhaps such expert testimony is not needed. Large numbers of Americans can add together some obvious facts and arrive at the dangers of obscenity. Such facts might include rising crime rates, particularly among juveniles, increased incidence of venereal disease, out-of-wedlock pregnancies, divorce. Ample studies have been made that demonstrate that overwhelming numbers of Americans engage in illicit sexual intercourse before, during, and after marriage. All of these increases have been coincident with the liberalized attitudes toward obscenity and the breakdown of censorship.

But such a statement has all the earmarks of a classic syllogism. If A (increased crime, etc.) is true and B (less censorship of obscenity) is true, therefore C (obscenity causes the increased crime) must be true. The problem with such reasoning is that other sets of facts could produce different or opposite conclusions. Such facts might include increased attendance at colleges and universities, art museums and concert halls, the number of nonviolent expressions of dissent, the opposition to the violence of the war in Vietnam, the interest of young people in religion, and the number of marriages. Since these have been coincidental with the rise of pornographic material, an opposite conclusion could be reached.

A number of efforts have been made over the years to discover scientifically whether or not pornographic material really does incite to sexual immorality and violence.

The research staff of the Commission on Obscenity and Pornography followed up the statement, quoted above, of Dr. Frignito. It studied 436 cases from his court and reported the following findings:

Of the offenses committed by these 436 juveniles, 92 per cent were classified as having no sex implication, 4 per cent were classified as implying some sexual activity (primarily in cases such as incorrigibles or runaways where the reason for complaints stemmed from sexual promiscuity), and 4 per cent were classified as sex-specific offenses.

The central variable of concern in the study was the presence or absence of exposure to pornography on the part of these delinquents. *There was absolutely no mention of pornography or erotica in any of the materials contained in the case records of any of these 436 juveniles.* [Their emphasis.] It is clear that the neuropsychiatric staff did not systematically enquire into this area. But it also seems that pornography is neither salient nor important enough to appear spontaneously in a probing examination of the background and circumstances of juvenile offenses.

This find is, to say the least, surprising, particularly since testimony before various Congressional Committees had led the researchers to believe that there would be at least some mention of pornography in the records of these juvenile delinquents.

The commission staff also studied 487 unwed pregnant teenagers at the Webster School in Washington, D. C. The girls, aged thirteen to eighteen, were "generally from large, lower-middle-class black families (many coming from broken homes), and were about average in intelligence. Test findings and interviews revealed that many of these girls were rather immature or unrealistic in their understanding of love and sexual behavior, and many apparently possessed a rather negative self-image in terms of their attractiveness as female figures."

The study showed that the girls "did practically no reading of erotic books." The researchers then inquired as to magazine reading, finding that "most of them did report reading about the sex scandals and romances contained in the popular 'confession' magazines often found in their homes. They indicated particular interest in the magazine articles and pictures concerning unusual births and premature babies."

The report continued:

> Musical records present quite a different picture from the one presented by reading matter. *All* [their emphasis] of the Webster School girls reported listening and dancing to rock and roll music, either with other girls or with boys. Since they rarely went to parties or went out in cars, one must conclude that most of the music was heard at home—either in the girls' or the boys' homes. The girls claimed that the rhythms and the lyrics frequently evoked romantic feelings which were sexually exciting, and that this arousal sometimes gave rise to sex play and love making. . . .
>
> By virtue of its seemingly universal appeal to adolescent females, one must recognize the significance of recorded music as an integral part of the social fabric of the adolescent subculture.

The research produced another, perhaps surprising, finding from interviews with these pregnant teenagers:

Many of the Webster School girls, in reporting the conditions and circumstances under which their first sexual intercourse took place, indicated that it occurred in front of a television set. Often, the girls found themselves alone with the boy either in their own or in the boy's home. Since the girls generally had difficulty in maintaining meaningful or satisfactory conversation with the boys, television served as a welcome substitute. Another common substitute for social conversation among heterosexual adolescent pairs is handholding and caressing. The romantic scenes portrayed on the television screen evoked feelings of love with its associated erotic component; this facilitated caressing, and sometimes culminated in sexual intercourse.

When asked to rank four media for sexual stimulation, the Webster girls ranked television first, records second, movies third, and books fourth. Lest this be seen as a universal condition, the research team also questioned junior college girls from upper-middle-class homes. They ranked movies first, books second, records third, and television fourth.

The results of the study are surprising. Among the unwed mothers, television, the most heavily censored medium, was the most erotically stimulating and phonograph records, which are perhaps the least censored, ranked second.

Concluded the researchers:

> Clearly the pregnant girls did not become pregnant as a result of exposure to obscene and pornographic materials. Rather, the stimuli which typically "turned them on" and which they labeled as erotically arousing were the ordinary forms of mass media to which practically all members of our culture are frequently exposed.

Such studies could be listed at great length. The end result of them would be that more studies are needed. No clear-cut evidence exists that pornography is either harmful to those who view it or totally without harmful effects. If no one-to-one relationship can be established between pornography and crime, neither can it be shown that pornography is terribly beneficial to those interested in it.

In another study, this one in San Francisco with findings corroborated in other cities, the Commission researchers turned up evidence that suggest that the harmful effects of pornography might well be discounted. Certainly it is true that the common public image of the pornography-viewer is incorrect.

Perhaps the most significant fact to emerge from this study is that the majority of consumers of erotica are middle-class, middle-aged, white males. The modal age group (57%) noted was between 26 and 45 years of age, with 20% in the 46 to 55 age group. Eighty-four per cent of the consumers had been to college; the predominant percentage (53%) had graduated. Only 16 per cent had had less than a high school education.

Occupational data revealed the largest single group (23.9%) to be mass white-collar workers (sales and service personnel, office staff and clerks); 18.7 per cent were professionally employed; 14.7 per cent in semi-professional work (social workers, teachers, etc.), and 11 per cent in a managerial staff or business ownership category. In all, a total of 69 per cent of consumers were either white-collar workers, managerial staff, professionals, or semiprofessionals. Data returned from observation of and interviews with patrons of theaters, arcades and bookstores revealed that over 70 per cent of the consumers were white and approximately 95 per cent were male. Interviews with patrons also demonstrated that at least 58 per cent were married and 20 per cent were single. . . .

Certain sources have suggested that the audience of erotica is essentially comprised of "perverted," "sick" individuals. It is interesting to note, however, that a considerable majority (62.5%) of movie theater patrons described themselves as totally heterosexual, 18.7 per cent as heterosexual with slight homosexual tendencies, 14.5 per cent as heterosexual with strong homosexual tendencies, and only 2.3 per cent as exclusively homosexual. In addition, when asked an open-end question as to what kinds of sexual behavior they most disapproved of, the largest group of respondents (12%) listed sado-masochism;

9.2 per cent homosexuality, 2.8 per cent bestiality, pedophilia and sodomy, and 8 per cent noted a combination of these.

Other information from the study is pertinent here. The preponderance (over 90 percent) of the consumers of pornography were leading "active and varied" sex lives. Most of the men said the pornography was "educational," "entertaining," "sexually satisfying in itself," or just something "to pass the time."

No one, particularly the commission, believes these studies are definitive. But they do shed important light on who consumes pornography and why. Preliminary though they are, these studies indicate that the widespread and common notions about pornography addicts and its effects may be partially incorrect. If pornography and obscenity cause a public menace by leading to crimes and antisocial behavior, then it is "middle-class, middle-aged, white males" that commit most of the crimes. A quick look at the population of penitentiaries indicates that this is not the common group from which convicts come. Therefore, some doubts, at least, may be cast upon the alleged dangers obscenity and pornography pose for society.

There is another line of argument, equally unproven, that suggests that obscenity and pornography may even be beneficial to society. Such a theory—and that is all it is—is rooted in the psychological nature of sexual relationships. Love, desire, anticipation, and other emotions that are psychological in nature are vital to the sexual process; sex is not solely a physical activity. Contrary to the phony sex portrayed in cheap novels and pornography, the psychological processes are particularly important for men. It is believed, for example, that no male can masturbate without engaging in fantasy. Men are aroused by the sight of a woman whom they consider attractive or by remembrances or photographs.

Therefore, according to this line of argument, pornography serves a useful function in society by abetting the psychological aspects of sex. The six million men and women who purchase *Playboy* magazine every month presumably find the photographs of breasts and buttocks pleasing, a balm to curiosity, or an inspiration to fantasy.

This argument has even been extended to the most disgusting types of pornography. Presumably, such material offers some measure of relief from sexual tension in its devotees. Indeed, Denmark, the only country where pornography is legal, had a *decline* in sex crimes since their law changed.

To repeat, all this is as much a theory as the contention that obscenity incites to crime. The possibly useful function of pornography could well be a subject for scholarly inquiry, however.

One final point must be made concerning the possible dangers of obscenity and pornography to society. Many have made it, but few as well as Professor Kristol in his *New York Times Magazine* article already cited. He pointed out that everyone recognizes limits on free or artistic expression. We would not permit a person actually to commit suicide on the stage or for actual torture to take place. He added: "And I know of no one, no matter how free in spirit, who argues that we ought to permit gladiatorial contests in Yankee Stadium, similar to those once performed in the Colosseum in Rome— even if only consenting adults were involved."

Professor Kristol suggested that bearbaiting and cockfighting are prohibited simply out of compassion for the suffering animals. "The main reason they were abolished," he wrote, "was because it was felt that they debased and brutalized the citizenry who flocked to witness such spectacles." He then arrived at this important point:

> And the question we face with regard to pornography and obscenity is whether . . . they can or will brutalize and debase our citizenry. We are, after all, not dealing with one passing incident—one book, or one play, or one movie. We are dealing with a general tendency that is suffusing our entire culture. . . .
>
> Pornography is not objectionable simply because it arouses sexual desire or lust or prurience in the mind of the

reader or spectator; this is a silly Victorian notion. A great many non-pornographic works—including some parts of the Bible—excite sexual desire very successfully. What is distinctive about pornography is that, in the words of D. H. Lawrence, it attempts "to do dirt on [sex] ... [It is an] insult to a vital human relationship."

In other words, pornography differs from erotic art in that its whole purpose is to treat human beings obscenely, to deprive human beings of their specifically human dimension.

If pornography and obscenity debase a human activity that clearly distinguishes man from other forms of animals, then is not man and his society demeaned by its presence?

Professor Kristol felt the demeaning of man through pornography and obscenity carried two dangers. First, it led men and women into an infantile expression of sex, making it more difficult for them to learn more mature and responsible attitudes. Second, he suggested there were important political ramifications for America. Simply stated, Kristol suggested that if our society is demeaned and made more sexually infantile through exposure to pornography, then we will be less able to govern ourselves effectively because of a loss of moral character.

One other point was made by Professor Kristol. The easing or discarding of censorship led to the publication of no significant body of previously suppressed literature. But, in his opinion, the commercialization of sex and pornography has kept many excellent books of important literary merit from being published because they do not deal with sex. Our literature is lessened by our emphasis on sex.

If it were agreed in America that pornography poses a present and latent danger to society and should be censored, there are still the practical difficulties of deciding what is to be censored and by whom. We have already encountered the difficulties in defining obscenity. If we are to have censorship, what is to be declared obscene? Hemingway's love scene between Maria and Jordan? *Playboy* magazine? A rape scene in a movie?

The decision of what is to be censored will probably be resolved by the question of who does the censoring. As the matter now stands, the Supreme Court serves as a national board of censors. It is a role rather reluctantly assumed, and one easily criticized. In a dissenting opinion in 1968, Justice Douglas remarked:

> Today this Court sits as the nation's board of censors. With all respect, I do not know of any group in the country less qualified first, to know what obscenity is when they see it, and second, to have any considered judgment as to what the deleterious or beneficial impact of a particular publication may be on minds either young or old.

There are those who disagree, maintaining that the term obscene is no more vague than many other legal concepts and that juries are just as capable of deciding what is obscene as they are in making judgments on other legal issues.

In his book, *The Smut Peddlers,* author James Jackson Kilpatrick stated this argument in these terms:

> For every sharp and cleanly delineated law, such as the law on honest weight, or the laws on speeding, or the laws that divide petit from grand larceny at the fifty-dollar mark, they (defenders of obscenity laws) cite a dozen statutes in which a jury's judgment, discretion and flexible interpretation spell the difference between guilt and innocence. What constitutes justifiable homicide? What constitutes non-negligent manslaughter? How is "consent" proved in a rape case? . . . What is simple negligence? What is gross negligence? Due care? The prudent man? Reasonable doubt? . . . What of the ten thousand individual and particular issues of due process? What constitutes a fair trial? . . .
>
> The law of obscenity is not different. The word "obscene" is a word of common usage. Jurors know what it means, precisely as they know what other elusive terms of the law mean —*to them.* [His emphasis] And if an obscenity law cannot be drafted as neatly as a speed-limit law, one ought not to complain excessively.

Perhaps, but such a system is too reminiscent of the days of Anthony Comstock, self-appointed censors, police raids, lurid trials, imprisonment for publishing *thoughts*. All this was declared unconstitutional once. It surely would be again, if we were to return to it.

There are more pragmatic difficulties. The United States would return to a system in which residents of one city or state were forbidden to read or view what was permitted in another. A book publisher or movie producer might be jailed in one community, while being praised in another. There would be no uniformity. Certainly the mere threat of being prosecuted somewhere would act as a drag on freedom of expression. Writers, publishers, and producers would inexorably be brought down to the standard of the most conservative and easily offended. Besides, the fact that juries make individual decisions in other legal matters is no recommendation, for even in other matters there is no uniformity. One jury convicts a man and another sets him free for essentially the same crime. It makes both law enforcement and corrections more difficult.

The difficulties may be illustrated by two rather celebrated court cases from the mid-1960s. In the first, publisher Ralph Ginzburg was convicted of twenty-eight counts of sending obscene materials through the mails, including a newsletter, a magazine, and a book. He was sentenced to five years in prison and was fined heavily.

The case went to the Supreme Court, which upheld his conviction and sentence in 1966. The high court's decision was based, not on the alleged obscenity of the materials, but on the advertising and promotion Ginzburg had used. Through use of such a postmark as Intercourse, Pennsylvania, and salacious advertisements, Ginzburg had, in the majority opinion, "pandered" his materials.

Ginzburg's conviction was roundly assailed in dissenting opinions and by liberal commentators ever since. The principal objection is that when Ginzburg advertised and mailed his materials, he had no way of knowing that it was or would be found illegal. Justice Douglas was particularly "shocked" that any man could be sent to prison for "publishing anything, especially tracts so distant from any incitement to action as" Ginzburg's.

The second case involved comedian Lenny Bruce. He was convicted in lower courts of performing an obscene nightclub act. The main objection was that he used a good bit of four-letter, biological profanity. The case was appealed through the courts until in 1966, the Supreme Court of the State of New York overturned the conviction, saying Bruce's act was not obscene because integral parts of it "included comments on the problems of contemporary society, religion, hypocrisy, racial prejudices and human tensions."

Unfortunately, the court decision came too late, for Lenny Bruce had died under conditions that made him a martyr to many people. Not content with his conviction, police and other censors had hounded Bruce through a form of blacklisting. Theater and nightclub managers received intimidating phone calls if they booked Bruce for appearances. He was driven from his livelihood and reduced to extreme poverty. Never a highly stable person, he was driven deeper into the use of drugs and alcohol. His health was broken and he did not live to see his vindication.

Insight into Bruce comes from his friend, writer John D. Weaver: "He was simply trying to explain that the truly offensive words of the twentieth century have nothing to do with copulation or defecation. Today's dirty words . . . are those that put a human being down because of his race, his religion or his national origins."

Bruce himself perhaps said it more succinctly, "What's wrong with appealing to prurient interest? We appeal to *killing* interest."

The practical difficulties of enforcing censorship of obscene materials were the main reason the Commission on Obscenity and Pornography recommended doing away with all attempts to censor. The difficulties and dangers of censorship outweighed the dangers of pornography. The report was promptly denounced by the White House and key members of Congress. It passed into that vast limbo populated with tens of thousands of little-read, unused studies.

It would seem, then, that an impasse, the point of agreeing to disagree, has been reached. It has been argued that both censorship and unrestrained pornography pose dangers for America.

But it seems that there is a way of looking at the problem that at least offers some hope of solution. It is possible that in this issue, as in so many others, we are attacking a twentieth-century problem with nineteenth-century ideas. We have tried crime and punishment, laws, censors, juries and jails, vigilante committees, persuasion and harassment of the dealers in smut. The record of success is not very good.

If it is agreed that pornography of the less savory varieties is unwanted, that it debases our society, that it is offensive to large numbers of Americans as an invasion of their privacy, then there are several ways to attack the problem other than by censorship.

For one, pornography could rather easily be regulated, licensed, and taxed. We do this with a host of other products and services (liquor, cigarettes, gambling), including some that are quite beneficial to society (private schools, nursing homes, elevators, restaurants, places of entertainment). It is at least reasonable that pornography could be similarly regulated. It could be decided, for example, that the sale of still or motion photographs of male and female genitalia should be licensed and taxed. Rules could be applied to the terms of sale, the nature of the premises, the methods of display of such material. It would be possible for such materials to be subject to special mailing rates.

There is some precedent for this. New York City, like many other places, has prohibited topless and bottomless waitresses by regulating the areas of the body that must be clothed. No great hue and cry was heard about censorship, nor was any great loss to the community deemed to have occurred.

There is still another way to minimize the distribution of pornography. Our society has potent mechanisms for combatting the socially undesirable or promoting the desirable. Through the years, we have campaigned against forest fires, reckless driving, venereal disease, juvenile delinquency, racial and religious prejudice, violence. We have supported church attendance, voting, the United Nations, God, country, motherhood, teachers, and policemen. The point is that our society has powerful means to combat anything that tends to demean society and dishonor women. The means include churches, the home, schools, youth groups, clubs and associations of all varieties, the police, and many government agencies. When the mass media and the advertising industry join in the effort, a remarkably powerful means of public education is developed. We have combatted or promoted a host of other ideas, but not one against obscenity and pornography.

Such a program need not recommend or even mention censorship. The campaign could aim, not at the point of sale, but at the point of purchase or use. The gist of the campaign might be that sex is an intensely private activity, an ennobling act of love and communication between two human beings. Love-making is part of what distinguishes man from other animals. Obsessive interest in the prurient might be pointed out to be juvenile, even infantile, a symptom of maladjustment, contributory to self-debasement, dangerous to society, and debilitating to women.

Such a campaign would not need to deal in specifics. A particular publication or movie need not be labeled as obscene. It could well be left to the individual to decide what he believes demeans himself and other human beings. But the effect might be increased understanding of and respect for the humanity of man. At the very least, such an effort could make obscenity and pornography as unfashionable as racial and religious prejudice.

There may be pitfalls in such a plan, but one point may be made with safety. We can more easily combat obscenity and pornography than we can censorship. Censorship by its very nature precludes even discussion of the forbidden subject. It is a cancerous growth that spreads throughout the world of ideas and information. It poses a threat to all our freedoms. Obscenity and pornography are also cancerous, but we have ways of exorcising them through regulation and public education. There is at least the possibility of curing the disease and saving the patient. Censorship, as the past shows, can be fatal.

# PART II

# Censorship of Information

# CHAPTER 8
# Secrecy in Government

In June of 1971, there burst upon the American scene something known as "The Pentagon Papers." In a sensation-loving country, they turned out to be a major sensation.

The Pentagon Papers were written in 1968 by the order of the then defense secretary, Robert McNamara. It is speculated, but hardly established, that Secretary McNamara ordered a study or history of America's involvement in the Vietnam War because of his growing disenchantment with the nation's role in the conflict.

Secretary McNamara's motives aside, forty writers were employed. To this day the identity, let alone the qualifications, of these writers is unknown to the general public. The writers were certainly diligent. They penned forty-seven volumes containing four million words (this book is only about fifty thousand words), tracing American involvement in the Vietnamese war from its earliest days shortly after World War II to 1968. At least some of the activities of Presidents Harry Truman, Dwight Eisenhower, John Kennedy, and Lyndon Johnson were described, as well as the ideas and information from a host of other military and government officials. The forty-seven volumes were loaded with memos, reports, and opinions from a variety of officials.

The Pentagon Papers were labeled a "history." But as such they were hardly scholarly. The authors were unknown. No interviews were conducted. The writers had access to only one source of information—the files of the Defense Department (the Pentagon) and it is not even known if they had access to all of them. They definitely did not make use of the files of the White House or the State Department, where important decisions in the war were made. At best the Pentagon Papers are important *evidence* for histories yet to be written.

The Pentagon Papers were compiled and a very limited quantity printed, reportedly only fifteen copies. All were labeled, supposedly by McNamara, "top secret-sensitive." This is about the highest form of government classification. It means the contents directly affect the nation's security and vital interest. Access to the information is severely restricted to those persons "cleared" through elaborate investigation. In effect this meant that hardly anyone outside of the government and few within it were to peruse this laboriously prepared "history." It was a federal criminal offense to reproduce or publish any of these papers.

Yet, large portions of the Pentagon Papers were photocopied and turned over in cloak-and-dagger fashion to selected newspapers known to be opposed to the war in Vietnam.

After weeks of intensive preparation, the *New York Times* began to publish excerpts from the purloined documents. The *Washington Post* and other newspapers shortly began to publish similar articles.

Aghast at the violation of the "top secret" stamp, the federal government, led by former Attorney General John Mitchell, sought court injunctions to prevent further publication of articles based upon the stolen documents. The *Times* and *Post* published only three installments before a temporary injunction was issued.

The newspapers fought the injunction on two major counts. First, the government's efforts to stop the publication was not only censorship of the press in violation of the First Amendment, it was *prior restraint*. This is an odious condition that keeps newspapers from printing material just because someone thinks it might be harmful. Second, there was nothing in the Pentagon Papers, let alone in those portions published, that was harmful to the vital interests of the nation. Embarrassing to past and present government officials, yes, but threatening to national security, no.

The issue went to the Supreme Court, which took hurried action. It decided six to three against the government and refused to stay publication of the articles. Three members of the majority based their decisions on the unconstitutionality of prior restraint of newspapers. Three others felt there was nothing in the documents to endanger the nation. The dissenting judges generally believed the newspapers had a responsibility to consult with the government before publication, reporting their possession of classified documents. They also objected to the haste with which the court had decided so important an issue. The court made it clear, however, that freedom to publish the documents did not absolve the newspapers from the risk of criminal prosecution for revealing classified government documents.

The Pentagon Papers and the controversy over their publication are important for several reasons. They constitute a report of how the nation stumbled into the longest and perhaps least liked war in its history. The Papers are fuel for the growing debate in Congress and in the nation over the war powers of the presidency and how these might be or should be curbed.*

More relevant to this book is what the Pentagon Papers revealed about the use of government classification of documents as a means of censorship. Government attorneys made repeated efforts before several judges to prove that "irreparable injury to the national defense" would result from publication of the Pentagon Papers. Some of the judges were clearly sympathetic to the argument. They were apparently fully pre-

* For a discussion of these issues read the author's *Presidential Power: How Much is Too Much?* (New York: McGraw-Hill, 1971).

pared to stop publication of any material injurious to the nation. Yet, the government failed repeatedly to convince the majority of the judges that the documents contained any material injurious to the national defense or any material that was more than embarrassing to certain officials.

The ultimate denial of the importance of the documents came from the government itself. After portions of the Pentagon Papers were published, nearly all the formerly "top secret" reports were declassified and sent to the printer for public distribution. In testimony before a Senate subcommittee, Harding Bancroft, executive vice-president of the *Times,* called the Pentagon Papers "a valid example of . . . classification overkill."

It is not difficult to understand why the documents were labeled "top secret" when they were written in 1968. The nation was deeply involved in an undeclared war, with hundreds of thousands of American troops committed in Southeast Asia. The American people were being asked to sacrifice these thousands of men, as well as inconvenience the lives of millions of others—not to mention spending tens of billions of tax dollars, which was causing a major inflation with serious repercussions for the American economy.

During one of the American-supported, South Vietnamese "raids" into North Vietnamese territory, enemy ships attacked American destroyers in the Gulf of Tonkin. American officials claimed later that these destroyers were not actively engaged in the South Vietnamese raids but were on an "intelligence gathering" mission—a euphemism for "spying." It is easily understandable that the North Vietnamese, being under attack, would think that the destroyers were involved.

The attack on the destroyers was subsequently presented to Congress by President Johnson as an unprovoked attack on American ships. As a result, Congress authorized the president to "take all necessary measures" to "repel" an attack against American forces in Vietnam. This "Gulf of Tonkin Resolution" became known as an "unofficial" declaration of war, although President Johnson insisted he had the powers to engage American forces even without the resolution.

The Pentagon Papers indicated that the United States propelled itself into the war on the basis of inconclusive evidence of Communist aggression; countered the efforts of the South Vietnamese to settle their dispute with the North through negotiation; bombed the North, as well as engaged in other military actions, which were of dubious value to begin with and continued them long after they were known to be of no value.

Particularly startling was the evidence of duplicity on the part of administration officials. President Johnson said he knew of no plans to enlarge the war into North Vietnam in June 1964, when, according to the Pentagon Papers, plans for "retaliatory actions" had been formulated. President Johnson denied that the sending of additional American troops to Vietnam constituted a change in policy, whereas the Pentagon Papers indicate that the troops were seen as the start of an American involvement in a land war in Asia, one that would be long and require still more troops.

There were several such instances. In President Johnson's 1964 campaign against Republican Senator Barry Goldwater, he attacked Goldwater for urging the bombing of North Vietnam. The Pentagon Papers reveal that plans for the Johnson administration to undertake such bombing had already been formulated. In February 1965, President Johnson was saying he wanted "no wider war" at a time when McGeorge Bundy, one of his key assistants, was urging a policy of "sustained reprisal" against North Vietnam.

Whatever the facts may be, the important points for this discussion are that vital information about what was happening in Vietnam was concealed from the American people in 1964 and 1965; that the needed information was further hidden behind a "top secret" stamp when the Pentagon Papers were compiled in 1968; and that the government, with a new president, sought further to keep the information from the public in 1971 by seeking to enjoin their publication in prestigious American newspapers.

To repeat, it was not difficult to see why the "top secret"

stamp was used to shield the American people from this information. Its effect was to undermine the trust of Americans in
the veracity of their elected and appointed federal officials—
an undesirable state of affairs, to say the least.

The Pentagon Papers were hardly an isolated example. A
disputed memorandum from a lobbyist for the International
Telephone and Telegraph Company was printed by columnist
Jack Anderson. It suggested that high Justice Department officials had granted a favorable settlement in an antitrust case
to the company in exchange for a very large contribution to
the Republican party to defray the expenses of its National
Convention in 1972. The officials denied the charges. Other
"leaked" information indicated that the same company had
sought to involve government officials in an attempt to overthrow a socialist government in Chile. Anderson also printed
minutes of a top-level National Security Council meeting purporting to show that President Nixon favored Pakistan in the
brief India-Pakistan War in 1972.

In his testimony before the Senate Subcommittee on Constitutional Rights of the 92nd Congress, Mr. Bancroft listed
these examples in which classification had thwarted the efforts
of *Times* reporters to gain information:

> Actual cases where our reporters have met official resistance
> have been in respect to such matters as the numbers of medals
> awarded to generals in Vietnam, the identities of contractors
> who are found to have made excessive profits by the Renegotia-
> tion Board, reports of government tests on consumer products,
> the intercession of members of Congress in the affairs of ad-
> ministrative and regulatory agencies, and so on.

Actually, the problem is more serious than Bancroft's examples. Congress, coequal with the executive branch and in
many ways (through taxation, for example) more powerful,
has great difficulty finding out what the executive branch is
doing. The Pentagon Papers are one example. Congress knew
nothing about them. Indeed, copies of the documents were not

sent to Congress until some time after they were printed in the press.

There are more serious instances. On December 21, 1970, the report of the Subcommittee on United States Security Agreements and Commitments Abroad of the Senate Foreign Relations Committee was released. The subcommittee, chaired by Senator Stuart Symington of Missouri, worked for almost two years. Its report may be considered a massive indictment of how the United States became involved in commitments to more than forty-three nations by "treaty and agreement" and operated "some 375 major foreign military bases and 3,000 minor military facilities spread all over the world."

The Symington subcommittee report is laced throughout with expressions of the difficulty the senators had in obtaining information about United States commitments abroad. Items:

• The committee traced the growth of American commitments following World War II. It included this paragraph:

In addition, primarily through Executive Agreements, the Administrations of Presidents Kennedy and Johnson undertook still additional arrangements. *Many of the latter were not publicly disclosed; some were kept from most if not all members of Congress.* [Emphasis added.]

• In the 1950s, treaties and agreements were reached with the Republic of the Philippines stating that "an armed attack on the Philippines could not but be also an attack upon the military forces of the United States." Said the subcommittee:

*In this case, as in others, neither the approval nor the consent of Congress was requested. Nor, in some respects was Congress informed until long after the fact."* [Emphasis added.]

• The subcommittee found that a secret agreement had been reached with South Korea to provide $140 million for new weapons as part of the price for the entry of South Korean troops into the war in Vietnam. Said the subcommittee:

*Congress knew nothing about the agreement at the time it was
made and learned about it later only with great difficulty.*
[Emphasis added.]

The full subcommittee report lists many other examples in
which "top secret" and "secret" labels were used to keep Congress and the people uninformed about American commitments abroad.

No thoughtful person in or out of Congress is suggesting
that the affairs of government be opened completely, free to
be scrutinized by all. Three general types of information are
considered in need of classification.

1. Information that is important to the nation's military
   security. Obvious examples would be defense plans in
   case the nation or its allies are attacked; types of weapons and their deployment; items of military intelligence
   about possible enemies; and much more. To make
   such information public would be to put the facts directly in the hands of actual or potential enemies. The
   strength of the nation would be diminished immeasur-
   ably.

2. Diplomatic messages between the United States and
   other countries. Full and candid exchange of points
   of view is important in diplomacy. Foreign diplomats
   simply will not be as frank if they believe their comments will be made public. *Their* national security
   might be endangered, and the leaders of those countries might be publicly embarrassed. In the United
   States, George Washington, as the first president, invoked the practice of making diplomatic messages secret.

3. In domestic affairs, it is often important to keep discussion secret, at least for a limited time. Again, full
   and frank discussion is hindered when participants believe everything they say may be made public.

Americans perhaps do not always realize it, but secrecy has long been considered vital in nongovernmental activities. It is an established fact that labor-management collective bargaining over wages cannot occur in a "goldfish bowl" of publicity. Negotiations occur in secret and are reported to the public when concluded. Indeed, nearly every organization, from simple clubs to giant industrial corporations, tries to maintain privacy, if not secrecy, concerning its policies, how they are arrived at, and how they are carried out.

The problem, then, is not that the federal government engages in secrecy about its affairs, but that it abuses it, engaging in censorship to deprive the people and their representatives in Congress of the information they need to participate in the affairs of the nation.

# CHAPTER 9
# How Washington Censors Information

A serious criticism of the federal government is that it deliberately overclassifies information to keep important facts from the public and from Congress.

Some revealing evidence of this was provided in June 1971 when a subcommittee of the House Committee on Government Operations heard William G. Florence, who has recently retired after forty-seven years as a top civilian security expert with the Department of Defense. He listed some "not very exceptional" and "quite common" examples of overclassification in the Pentagon.

> Some time ago, one of the service Chiefs of Staff wrote a note to the other Chiefs of Staff stating briefly that too many papers were being circulated with the top secret classification. He suggested that use of the classification should be reduced. Believe it or not . . . that note itself was marked "top secret."
>
> The Air Force Electronics Systems Division at Hanscom Field, Massachusetts, adopted the following statement for use on selected documents: "Although the material in this publication is unclassified, it is assigned an overall classification of confidential". . .

Not very long ago, someone in the Navy Department placed the "secret" marking on some newspaper items of particular interest to the Navy. Subsequently, that action caused some embarrassment to the Department of Defense. As a result, a special directive had to be published to tell people not to classify newspapers.

The humorousness of these examples contrasts with the more serious repercussions of overclassification. The Symington subcommittee was among those not amused.

The Executive Branch consistently over-classified information relating to foreign policy that should be a matter of public record. This is partly the result of bureaucratic timidity, especially at the middle and lower levels, where the prevailing approach is to look for some reason either to cover up or to withhold facts.

The subcommittee concluded that sometimes foreign policy information is classified at the request of foreign governments.

The Government of Thailand did not want it known that the United States was using air bases in that country. The Government of Laos did not want it known that the United States was fighting in a major fashion in that country. Even in the Philippines where there is a free press and a highly articulate political opposition, the Government of the Philippines did not want it known that the United States was paying heavy allowances to the Philippine non-combat contingent that went to Vietnam.

But the classification is often placed by American officials. Reported the subcommittee:

Classification often permits an ambiguity about various commitments to be purposely developed by the Executive Branch. The practice often is to:
Maximize commitment in secret discussion with foreign

governments; then minimize the risk of commitment in statements made to the American public. Maximize in public the importance of our friendly relationship and cooperation with a foreign government; then minimize, and often classify, that government's obstructiveness, failures and noncooperation.

In the subcommittee's view, America is "becoming an increasingly closed government," the antithesis of an "open society."

There is no merit to the argument that certain activities must be kept secret because a foreign government demanded they would be kept secret. Such a policy involves the Government of the United States in a web of intrigue which is alien to American traditions.

As examples, the subcommittee listed the classifications of America's multimillion dollar support of a 30,000-man Laotian army and the activity by American military units in Laos.

The result of such effort to classify over here information that is available to the public overseas has contributed to a growing discontent among the American people as to the credibility of their own government.

The executive branch penchant for practicing "secrecy from Congress" was criticized by the subcommittee. "It was with great surprise . . . that the subcommittee found, when it began its hearings, that at the direction of the Executive Branch there was to be no discussion of nuclear weapons overseas."

After prolonged discussion, the committee was granted a one-day briefing on the weapons. Only one copy of the transcript was to be made and it was to be held in the State Department.

Attempts have been made to estimate how much government material is "overclassified." A most revealing attempt was made by Arthur J. Goldberg before the House subcommittee (chaired by William S. Moorhead of Pennsylvania). As secretary of labor in the Kennedy administration, associate justice of the Supreme Court, and ambassador to the United Nations in the Johnson administration, he had a great deal of experience with classified documents. He told the Moorhead subcommittee:

> I have read and prepared countless thousands of classified documents. In my experience, 75 per cent of these documents should never have been classified in the first place; another 15 per cent quickly outlived the need for secrecy; and only about 10 per cent genuinely required restricted access over any significant period of time.

During the 1950s, a group of naval officers told Congress that an estimated 90 to 95 percent of the government's classified information was overclassified or needlessly classified.

How does so much overclassification of documents occur? For revealing answers, we must return to Mr. Florence's testimony before the Moorhead subcommittee.

One reason for overclassification, he suggested, is the existence of too many classifiers. In the Department of Defense, he said, authority to classify rests with the Secretary of Defense, who then directly assigns classification authority to a limited number of people. Mr. Florence estimated perhaps three hundred individuals. They in turn delegate their authority until "hundreds of thousands" of classifiers are to be found in the Pentagon. "Under this concept of derivative authority to classify, anyone can assign classifications, sir. Anyone."

Mr. Florence emphasized this statement, saying that "in the past several years I have not heard one person in the Department of Defense say that he had no authority to classify information."

It is the attitudes of the individual classifiers that are responsible for the reasons that material is or is not classified. One attitude is that material must be classified until reason is provided that it not be. Mr. Florence spoke of such documents as being "born classified." A related attitude is that material must not be declassified until there are no objections by anyone to its being released. Another attitude is that although suspect material may in itself not need to be classified, it might have some possible relationship to other materials that should be classified.

Mr. Florence sought to illustrate these attitudes:

> . . . I have received correspondence from the Air Force Systems Command objecting to possible declassification of items of information unless it could be proved to them that declassification would actually benefit the Air Force.
>
> More recently, I attempted to obtain concurrence of an air staff officer in declassifying the external view of fire control equipment being sold to Japan for use on the Japanese F-4 aircraft. In addition to other reasons for declassification that I was sponsoring, more than 12 of these sets had been lost in foreign territory. But I was told that concurrence could not be given until there is positive proof that possible enemy countries have had access to this system.

Mr. Florence said he ultimately prevailed and the information was declassified. Another example:

> Nearly two years ago, a West Coast firm published as unclassified a document describing their privately developed electronic system for air surveillance of missile sites. After considerable effort in obtaining a Government license for export, the company distributed the document last year, as unclassified, to numerous foreign countries. Of course, it had wide distribution in this country. Late in 1970, the Army came into possession of the company's information. In December, the Army sent a letter to the Defense Supply Agency in Los Angeles advising that the information required the classification "secret-Noforn." Mr. Chairman, "Noforn" is an acronym for "no foreign dissemination." The Defense Supply Agency was to conduct an inquiry into the purported "security violation." Incidentally, the Army letter itself contained information marked as confidential.

A final example. Mr. Florence described a proposal made in April 1970, by a Dr. Foster, a ranking Pentagon official, that with very few exceptions all material was to be declassified after two years. This was to be a step "toward actually eliminating overclassification and unnecessary classification of research and development information." Mr. Florence then said:

> This proposal for automatic declassification of research and development information after two years . . . [was] beaten down by objections from the pro-classification people in the department. It seemed that many people would have lost some of their classification prerogatives. I personally thought that Dr. Foster should have been awarded the highest of honors for the proposals that he made.

Another reason for overclassification is that the classifiers are given incentives to classify and are punished for failure to classify. Mr. Florence testified:

> To my knowledge, no one in the Department of Defense was ever disciplined for classifying information, regardless of how much the classification cost for unnecessary security protection or what damage resulted from the restriction against releasing the information to the public. But I have seen how rough a person can be treated for leaving classification markings off of information which he knows to be officially unclassified if someone "up the line" thinks that a classification should have been applied.

There are other problems with censorship through classification, in addition to the overuse of it. Classified material has a way of being "leaked" to Congress, the press, and the public. This undermines the entire classification system and leads to the conclusions that classification doesn't mean much anyway and that everyone can decide what should or should not be made public. Former Justice Goldberg described an example in testimony before the House:

On March 15, 1968, when I was Ambassador to the United Nations, I made certain major policy recommendations relating to the cessation of bombing of North Vietnam in a cable to the President. My memorandum was marked for the eyes of the President, Secretary of State, and Secretary of Defense only. It had a high security rating. . . .

Through no disclosure of my own, this document has in recent months been discussed in two books of general circulation authored by former Government officials, and was the subject of comment by President Johnson in a television interview. Although its words may technically still remain classified, its substance has been disclosed and, I must say, without injury to any national security or diplomatic interest. Some of those with access to it have described it publicly, but the Congressman and the citizen, the scholar and the critic, the journalist and the student—all who wish to know what their Government has done and rightly so—are presumably still denied the right to see the document.

Classified documents are leaked in three major ways. One is in the memoirs and other writings of government officials. Former presidents, cabinet officers, generals, White House aides, and others who were briefly at the apex of government tell their stories, making frequent, even generous use of still legally classified material. Such officials are making a judgment that the material should never have been or need not now be censored from the public and/or that the public need to know the information overrides its need for classification.

Second, classified information is frequently and deliberately leaked to newsmen. This process was described by columnist Max Frankel of the *New York Times:*

The government and its officials regularly and customarily engage in a kind of ad hoc, de facto "declassification" that normally has no bearing whatever on considerations of the national interest. To promote a political, personal, bureaucratic or even commercial interest, incumbent officials and officials who return to civilian life are constantly revealing the secrets entrusted to them. They use them to barter with Congress or the press, to curry favor with foreign governments and officials from whom they seek information in return. They use them freely, and with a startling record of impunity, in their memoirs and other writings.

If a government official believes that his point of view on a public question or his opposition to an existing policy or his personal importance can be furthered by revealing information, the fact of its classification need not and frequently does not stand in his way. He need only make the information known "off the record," leaving the willing newsman to attribute it to a "White House," "Pentagon," "State Department" or some other source, even a "high government official."

Again the justification for this is that the classification was unnecessary or that the need for the public was greater than the need for secrecy.

The third way, recently made famous, is for the documents to be stolen and turned over to the press, members of Congress, and presumably anyone else in the United States or abroad. The theft can be accomplished by anyone who has access to the documents and a photocopying machine. Motives for such action can include the monetary gain of selling them, altruistic belief that the documents should be made public, and the simple spite of a disgruntled public servant.

The newsmen and editors who receive the purloined information then decide whether they believe the information deserves secrecy or should be declassified by them and published.

There are pitfalls with such a system, aside from the joke they make of the federal system of classification. The declassification decisions are made ad hoc by people who are far from acquainted with the importance of the information. The facts or opinions revealed through the process are by their nature self-serving. They either bolster the person revealing the information or enable him to punish someone. In neither case is complete, well-rounded information made available to the public and Congress.

Such processes make newsmen, columnists, broadcasters, and editors the deciders of what the national interest is. The method undermines the nation's entire security system and heightens the dangers classification is supposed to alleviate. Peter F. Krogh, dean of the Georgetown University School of Foreign Service, wrote eloquently about this in a letter to the *Washington Post* in February 1972.

> Such practice, if pursued and indulged further, will give every government official license to be a free agent, enabled if not actually encouraged to undermine secretly . . . decisions with which he may personally disagree. It virtually invites officials to indulge frustration and resentment with impunity, under the guise of moral righteousness. Orderly administration can literally break down in these circumstances.
>
> I cannot, in short, emphasize too strongly that the practice of leaking secret documents, and its indulgence by the press, will rapidly lead to a crippling, not a strengthening, of the decision making process, and a deterioration rather than an improvement in the quality of our foreign policy. Deception and covering-up may be real concerns, but the answer to these ills is hardly to resort to a practice that can be equally pernicious in its total effect.

There are ways that federal officials censor information other than through the formal procedures of classification. Some of these were described by Lee White, former chairman of the Federal Power Commission, before the Moorhead subcommittee:

> Unfortunately, there is a tendency on the part of the Executive, and I think probably this is universal, to engage in gamesmanship in this whole field of making information available. Included in this category are "the stall," "the deluge of material," the selection of the day after Thanksgiving for release of documents, the please-be-more-specific dodge, and a host of others that innovative participants in the game can devise. There should be a conscious and conscientious effort to

avoid this temptation, for the issues involved and the princi-
ples involved are really quite serious.

I don't know the solution truly, but I can tell you as a participant in the game that I have done it, and there are times
when your mind begins to think more in terms of winning a
point than in the substances of what you are involved with.

The "point" to be won in the game Mr. White was talking
about is the concealment of information that the public is legally entitled to know. Other descriptions of these devices for
hiding information were given in testimony by Peter Schuck,
an attorney associated with the organization of consumer advocate Ralph Nader. His descriptions of the delaying tactics
are explanatory and need no illustration. He spoke of the
"fob-him-off-with-a-meaningless-summary" stratagem or the
"delay-until-the-information-becomes-stale" routine. Another
method of hiding information he called the "it's-exempt-be-
cause-it's-embarrassing" approach. If all else fails, he said, the
"sue-us-again" tactic is used. If the person wants the information, he will simply have to go to court to get it.

Any newsman and probably many members of Congress
who have ever tried to deal with governmental bureaucratic
agencies can testify that they have encountered such tactics
and have found them both infuriating and even more effective
than classification as a means of censorship. By delay, adher-
ence to pettifogging rules, and deliberate noncooperation,
even the most minor public officials can keep unwanted or
embarrassing information from the public.*

A final method of censorship to be discussed here, one
with far more notoriety, is "executive privilege." This is the
principle that the president cannot be required by judicial process to perform any given act and cannot, therefore, be re-

* One method revealed in the news involves overcharging for information.
A nominal charge is normally imposed by federal agencies for locating and
copying requested information. The Department of Agriculture, in 1972,
imposed a charge of six dollars per copy for several thousand reports sought
by the Nader organization. Other federal officials figured that a charge of
seventy-five cents for each item would have been appropriate.

quired to make information available to the Congress that he does not wish to divulge. Executive privilege is as old as the republic.

The system is based on the separation of powers in American government as provided for in the Constitution. The legislative, executive, and judicial branches are equals. Each has specific powers derived from the Constitution. If the president could be called before Congress or one of its committees to be questioned about his actions or lack of them or could be compelled to provide certain information wanted by Congress, then the office of president would lose dignity, the independence of the office would be lessened, and the separation of powers would be damaged.

The problem with executive privilege, certainly in the last few decades, is that powers of the executive branch have grown disproportionately to those of Congress. The president commands a military force of millions of men. He oversees the spending of hundreds of billions of dollars a year of tax money appropriated by Congress. He supervises a civilian work force of nearly three million men and women. He has almost sole conduct of American foreign policy and indeed has led the nation into wars in Vietnam and Korea and into other warlike actions without benefit of a declaration of war from Congress. Not the least is the tremendous audience the president commands when speaking on national television or in releasing statements to reporters.

If the president cannot be questioned about what he is doing—and much of what he is doing is classified as secret— then Congress can be expected to experience some difficulty in finding out what is going on and in exercising its own powers granted by the Constitution. There is a fear that presidents and their spokesmen reveal that which is favorable and hide the unfavorable. Some would say the Pentagon Papers are a record of presidential and executive branch deception of Congress and the people.

As now practiced, executive privilege is a bit confusing. Although the president cannot be made to testify or provide information to Congress and can refuse to allow members of his personal White House staff to testify, cabinet officers, department heads, bureau chiefs, and officials of regulatory agencies are permitted to testify and provide the information Congress desires. But there is a flaw in this system because the president is allowed to prevent these executive branch officers from divulging information that he does not want made known. In short, it is not possible to query the president through his subordinates. What he says to others and they say to him is privileged information.

Executive privilege is an awesome power, but presidents do not usually abuse it. President Nixon has been particularly troubled with it, because of the nature of his administration. He has the largest White House staff in history and makes extensive use of it in running the government. The most notable example is his presidential assistant Dr. Henry Kissinger. Dr. Kissinger is the most powerful man in the administration, next to the president, in the field of foreign affairs. He obtains, screens, and presents information to the president and advises him on policies. He communicates with foreign governments as a diplomat, makes frequent trips to foreign capitals, and accompanies the president on his trips abroad. He is involved in most of Mr. Nixon's top level foreign policy actions. Dr. Kissinger was dispatched both to Peking and Moscow to pave the way for the president's trips to China and Russia in 1972.

The less than sensible, and to members of the Senate Foreign Relations Committee infuriating, situation has developed wherein Dr. Kissinger briefs members of the press and foreign diplomats on American foreign policy and attempts to assuage senatorial feelings by holding private briefings with members of Congress, but is prevented by executive privilege from appearing before a Congressional committee. Members of Congress ask how they can fulfill their duties in the field of foreign policy when the key architect of presidential policy cannot be questioned.

But executive privilege has two faces, for in addition to the great power the president derives from it, when he uses it, particularly if he uses it too often, he is suspected of having something to hide. Talk of the "credibility gap" is heard and the standing of the president with the people may be damaged. Former commissioner White remarked before the Moorhead committee:

> . . . far more important is whether the President can invoke the privilege and convince the general public that his grounds for doing so are legitimate, reasonable, and convincing. May I say I think that is perhaps the most important sentence in my entire statement.

Thus, through formal classification of documents, bureaucratic footdragging, and executive privilege, a formidable apparatus for censoring the news available to the people and Congress has come to exist. It should be added that censorship is not just a phenomenon of the executive branch. Congress hides information through executive sessions of committees where the press is excluded and no records are kept, as well as in informal discussions in "cloakrooms" and other nonpublic places. A case could be and has been made that Congress engages in more secrecy than the White House.

The subcommittee headed by Representative Moorhead was hearing testimony regarding the effectiveness of and the need for revisions of the Freedom of Information Act of 1966, which had been enacted following extensive hearings. Its passage had been saluted by President Johnson and others as a form of guarantee that the American people and Congress would have full access to all information except that which was essential to the nation's defense.

Five years later, the Moorhead committee was hearing testimony about the ineffectiveness of the act and its need for revision. The subcommittee heard many of the ways, some of which were described here, that both the letter and the spirit of the act were violated. The Pentagon Papers were living proof that the United States did not have the freedom to disseminate information.

A succession of presidents have also tried to cope with the problem of unnecessary secrecy. President Nixon has been the most recent. On March 8, 1972, he issued an executive order to take effect June 1, 1972. Its aim was "to lift the veil of secrecy which now enshrouds altogether too many papers written by employees of the federal establishment." Some of the major features of the order were:

• A speed-up in the State Department's publication of its "Foreign Relations" series, reducing the time lag for the publication of diplomatic documents from twenty-six to twenty years within three years.

• The number of agencies allowed to use the "top secret" stamp was reduced from twenty-four to twelve and the number of individuals authorized to use the classification was cut to 1,860 from 5,100.

• Materials may be classified top secret, secret, or confidential only if their unauthorized disclosure "could reasonably be expected" to damage the nation's security.

• Officials who overclassify a document will be identified and will be subject to official reprimand.

• Unless specifically exempted, all top secret documents will be downgraded to "secret" after two years, to confidential after two more years, and declassified after a total of ten years. If originally classified secret, a document will be declassified after eight years. If originally confidential, only six years need elapse before declassification.

• Exceptions to these rules were specified. Any document exempted from automatic declassification will be subject to mandatory review after ten years. If still classified after thirty years, it will be automatically declassified unless the head of the originating agency directs in writing that it remain classified.

• An interagency classification review committee operating under the National Security Council will continuously monitor enforcement of the president's order.

At this writing no one knows how effective the new executive order will be. It was quickly pointed out that many of the problems uncovered by the Moorhead subcommittee would remain untouched. If the Pentagon Papers had been written under this order, most of them would still not be declassified as they are only six years old. Some people doubt whether the president has legal authority to issue such an order.

Other suggestions for obtaining information from the executive branch were made by Lee White, the former Federal Power commissioner. He suggested, first, that a concurrent resolution passed by large majorities of both Houses of Congress would make it extremely difficult for a president to refuse the information requested in the resolution.

Second, he suggested that members of Congress take court action to obtain information from executive departments when they believed the Freedom of Information Act had been violated. Such actions have already been initiated.

Mr. White believed that Congress could, third, take steps to be open about its own proceedings, thus making a contrast with some executive agencies.

The question of freedom of information is not just a woolly-headed exercise in liberty, but a concept that is important to the American democracy. Censorship of information does reflect on our attitudes toward government. But we must postpone this important matter until we consider the role of the nation's press in the question of information.

# CHAPTER 10
# Censorship of Newspapers

FREEDOM of information in America means, in large measure, freedom of the press.

For this discussion, the broadest possible meaning is being put upon the word "press." It includes newspapers, magazines, and books insofar as they deal with information about America and its problems, and with broadcast journalism on radio and television.

The press plays an important role in American self-government. It is a vital source of information about American problems, and what government is doing, not doing, and perhaps ought to do. Americans may not fully realize how much they depend on "news," whether written or broadcast, for the information necessary for any type of self-government.

The press also performs the function of "loyal opposition." The British have a more clear-cut scheme for such opposition. The part out of power, be it Labour or Conservative, maintains a "shadow cabinet" in the House of Commons. Every Friday that Commons is in session, government officers, including the prime minister, are closely questioned by members of the shadow cabinet and by any other member of Commons in order to develop clear-cut statements of policy.

In the United States, the function of the press is to question, pry, and criticize government actions and inactions. It can sometimes reach individuals Congress cannot, because of executive privilege. The press can also send reporters directly to the scene to obtain information, which may and frequently has conflicted with the official version.

The loyal opposition function of the press has long brought it into conflict with government officials. Every president including George Washington was plagued by a "hostile" press. During the administration of the second president, John Adams, the infamous Alien and Sedition Acts were passed, in part to muzzle the press.

Yet, the struggle between the press and government today seems as bad as or worse than ever in history. The press came under sharp attack from Vice-President Spiro T. Agnew and other officials of the Nixon administration. In a celebrated speech in November 1969, Mr. Agnew spoke of the "trend toward the monopolization of the great public information vehicles and the concentration of more and more power in fewer and fewer hands." He singled out the Washington Post Company, which owns the *Washington Post, Newsweek* magazine, and a television station and radio station. He contended that all four "harken to the same master." He accused the press of having "grown fat and irresponsible." He used such words as "beyond fair comment and criticism" and "excessive and unjust" criticism and "blind acceptance of their own opinions" in criticizing the nation's press.

Reporters charge that the government invokes censorship through classification, makes information difficult to obtain, and sometimes supplies incomplete or false information with the intent to "manage" the news. In the eyes of the press, the misleading of the press is the misleading of the people.

Why is there a great conflict between government officials and the press? A major reason is the tremendous growth in the size and power of the federal government, particularly the executive branch. "Uncle Sam" is by far the largest raiser of tax revenue. The federal government spends about 10 percent of all the money, private and public, expended in the United States. It influences in large and intimate ways nearly all the activity of every American. It is impossible in this book to detail the immense activities and influence of the federal government. To appreciate that influence, consider only the federal role in such a small matter as the control of pornography.

The increase in the power of the federal government since the 1930s has led to tremendous increase in the power of the president. As commander in chief of the armed forces and as "chief diplomat," the president has direct charge of the nation's immense involvement in world affairs. He collects taxes, prepares the budget, and spends the money. He administers the nation's laws. The president of the United States is widely acknowledged to be the single most powerful individual in the world, and a case can be and has been made that he is the most powerful individual, whoever holds the office, that the world has ever known.

Yet this power, great though it is, is constricted. According to the Constitution, his power is limited by Congress and the courts. There is also a practical limitation. A president can personally give attention to only a tiny portion of his domain. He must delegate his power and authority to tens, perhaps hundreds of thousands of other government officials, only some of whom he appoints. These "bureaucrats" have their own fiefdoms of power. They can ignore presidential wishes and engage in a variety of "foot-dragging" so as to thwart a president's aims. Consider only the actualities of classification of documents in the Pentagon, as described by Mr. Florence in Chapter 9, with the lofty goals set forth by presidents and Congresses.

Finally, a president is limited by his popular support among the people. It is axiomatic that if a majority or even a determined minority of the people do not want or do not approve of a presidential action, he will encounter great difficulty. The most recent example, often cited, is the opposition to the "escalation" of the war in Vietnam during the Johnson administration. It is widely believed that Mr. Johnson was forced to retire from office because of opposition to his war policy.*

In his penetrating and influential book, *Presidential Power*, written in 1960, Professor Richard E. Neustadt saw presidential power resting on the president's ability to influence one or both of two areas, the Washington community of congressmen, bureaucrats, and lobbyists, and the people. The two are separate, but not entirely distinct. A president's influence in the insular community of Washington depends in large measure on his knowledge of how things get done in Washington and his ability to get them performed through inspiration, persuasion, administrative skill, and political force. But part of the president's influence in Washington is derived from his popularity among the majority of the voters and their confidence in him, his judgment, and his actions.

Mass communications—particularly radio and television —have provided presidents with a tremendous opportunity to be seen and heard by the people. As president, a person can commandeer "prime" time on radio and television to explain his programs in any manner he sees fit and believes will lead to public support for these programs.

But the press can also use mass communication. The microphone, the camera, the teletype, and the jet plane have enabled reporters to visit the newsworthy trouble spots of the world and quickly describe and *show* the American people what is happening. Television news brings war, riots, floods, famine, and other distant events directly into the living rooms of Americans. Newsmen using print have been far more able to tell Americans in depth what is transpiring.

What the camera shows and reporters learn on the scene often conflicts with what the president or his aides say happened. To give only one of a large number of possible examples, in 1965 President Johnson sent American troops into the

* For a fuller account of these matters, read the author's *The American Political System* (New York: Parents Magazine Press, 1972).

Dominican Republic. In explaining his action to the American people, Mr. Johnson said in a nationwide television address on June 17:

> Some 1,500 innocent people were murdered and shot, and their heads cut off, and six Latin American embassies were violated and fired upon over a period of four days before we went in. As we talked to our ambassador to confirm the horror and tragedy and the unbelievable fact that they were firing on Americans and the American embassy, he was talking to us from under a desk while bullets were going through his windows and he had a thousand American men, women and children assembled in the hotel who were pleading with their President for help to preserve their lives.

Most American newsmen on the scene reported that no embassy had been fired upon, no one had been beheaded, no considerable loss of life was visible, and no American civilian was hurt.

Such incidents have helped to create what is now known as the "credibility gap," the tendency of members of the press, if not the public as well, to question and sometimes downright disbelieve presidential statements.

Thus, a conflict is joined between the presidents' need to gain public support for their policies and actions so they can be effective in the White House and the belief of the press that its most important function is to ferret out and report the truth.

The conflict becomes complex. Print and broadcast journalists feel that they are under pressure to counter presidential statements deliberately. There is a tendency in news columns to question the president's political opponents for their views on what the chief executive had to say. In editorials and news analysis articles, journalists strive to present other views and to criticize the president's arguments—all as a means of opposition to the president's powerful source of publicity.

The personalities and mental attitudes of newsmen often enter this conflict. By the very nature of his job, the good newsman has a need to question, to probe, to seek more facts. In his work, at least, he tends to be quarrelsome, iconoclastic as regards the powerful and famous, and somewhat fearless in his obstreperousness. But his ambitiousness can also interfere. As a newsman, his paycheck, career advancement, and esteem of his colleagues rest on his ability accurately to report the news and that includes unearthing some facts that public officials did not want known.* Thus, good newsmen—and there are many who are not—have a built-in thrust toward dissent. This is bound to make them less than popular with public officials, particularly with those who have something to hide.

The role of the press in informing the public and criticizing officeholders has been made more difficult by the drastic reduction in competition among the press.

Newspapers are a commercial enterprise, dependent upon advertising and circulation for a profit. After World War II, newspaper publishing turned into a highly unprofitable business. The rise of television drained off a significant amount of advertising. At the same time the costs of publishing, as reflected in wages, newsprint, printing, photoengraving, and delivering newspapers, rose sharply. Major American dailies folded by the hundreds until there are only a handful of cities with competing daily newspapers under separate ownership. The city of New York today has only two morning and one afternoon newspapers of metropolitan coverage.

There has been a rise in the numbers of smaller suburban weekly and daily newspapers. But these have small staffs and are able to give only limited coverage of national news.

Today there are 892 television and 6,976 radio stations, far more than the 1,766 daily newspapers. The radio and tele-

---

* An unfortunate example of this came from columnist Jack Anderson. In a radio broadcast he reported that Senator Thomas Eagleton of Missouri, whom Democratic nominee George McGovern had first chosen as his vice-presidential running mate, had a record of arrests for drunken driving. The report proved false, and Anderson admitted it, citing "deadline pressures" as his reason for making the mistake. This is another way of saying that Anderson was so eager for a "scoop" and "exposé" that he did not check his facts. This, of course, is a cardinal sin for a journalist.

vision stations, like the newspapers, are seldom able to cover directly any but local news. The broadcast medium, too, depends upon national news sources. For the most part this means the same sources—Associated Press and United Press International—as the newspapers. The three radio and television networks, CBS, NBC, and ABC, maintain their own reportorial staffs, generating some of their own news. These staffs cover and report the national and some international news that is carried on network news programs.

It is possible to make a rather short but complete list of the sources for national and international news. The two wire services and the three broadcasting networks, which also depend in large measure upon the two wire services. The three major weekly newsmagazines, *Newsweek, Time,* and *U. S. News and World Report,* maintain staffs of reporters at home and abroad. The *New York Times* and *Washington Post* also have sizable overseas staffs, and their reports are syndicated to other newspapers. Operating smaller national and international staffs are the *Baltimore Sun, Los Angeles Times,* and a few other papers, along with the major newspaper chains owned by Hearst, Knight, Newhouse, and Scripps-Howard. This is not a very long list. For practical purposes, the two wire services, three broadcasting networks, and the *Times* and *Post* are the major sources of the comprehensive, day-to-day news Americans receive.

A large number of journalists are assigned to cover White House activity. But this does not belie the central fact that such coverage is limited. Most of these reporters represent small daily or weekly newspapers or chains and the foreign press. Coverage tends to be sporadic rather than comprehensive and is often aimed at matters of particular local interest. Indeed, the large number of White House correspondents has made the presidential news conference largely a theatrical exercise. The president makes a statement and answers a few questions of his own choosing.

Because of the limited sources of national and international news, reporters make a considerable effort to be as complete, accurate, and unbiased as possible. At their best, which is most of the time, the reporters do this extremely well, maintaining a high level of objectivity in their reporting. Journalists, however, feel a need to do more than just report the news. Americans seem to want to know not just what the news is but what it means. The popularity of *Time* and similar magazines, as well as of the various columnists, who interpret and comment upon the news as well as report it, has led to the rise of interpretive reporting.

Such reporting requires a different type of newsman—one who is more analytical, informed, and specialized in some area of the news. Editorial comment, except in those rare instances in which a well-informed staff of editorial writers is employed, tends to lose importance.

Conflict between the press and the president is perhaps inevitable. It has been particularly notable in the administrations of Presidents Johnson and Nixon. Mr. Nixon sharply curtailed his number of press conferences; Mr. Agnew made his extremely critical speeches; the Nixon administration went to court to try to block publication of the Pentagon Papers.

There were other incidents of government-press conflict, not all involving the president. The FBI was asked to investigate CBS newsman Daniel Schorr. The investigation was called off, following adverse publicity. Grand juries and other investigative bodies sought to subpoena the notes and other records of reporters and to force them to testify about what they considered confidential information. Police and other investigators were found to be using fraudulent press cards as a means of gaining entry into radical, student, and similar organizations.

These skirmishes in the conflict between the press and government led the Constitutional Rights Subcommittee of the Senate, chaired by Senator Sam J. Ervin, Jr., to begin hearings on freedom of the press as guaranteed by the First Amendment. Many distinguished witnesses from the press and broadcast industry testified.

The hearing room rang with testimonials of the value of

the press and its role in America and the need to keep it un-
fettered to perform its function. There were many quotations
to this effect, including the one from Thomas Jefferson, which
Senator Ervin used at the outset of his remarks opening the
hearings: "No government ought to be without censors and
where the press is free, no one ever will."

The substance of the testimony before the subcommittee
was that the press can remain free, with great lip service being
paid to its "freedom," yet be hindered by very practical obsta-
cles in its path.

One of the fears was expressed by Mr. Bancroft of the
*New York Times,* who was quoted previously. He pointed out
that the government's court case did block publication of the
Pentagon Papers for fifteen days. He called this an "extremely
unfortunate precedent." He said the court action was the first
time in America that the federal government sought a "direct
suppression of the news." He expressed fear that the government may seek "similar restraints" in the future and declared
this "a prospect with which the nation's press cannot easily
live." He went on:

> . . . there is the danger that this unfortunate precedent will
> indeed have a chilling effect on the reporting of sensitive mat-
> ters and will deter reporters from conducting the kinds of
> thorough investigations which responsible journalism requires.
> A reporter, who, in the past, routinely checked his facts with
> government officials might well think twice before doing so,
> always fearful that by revealing his knowledge he will put into
> motion the government censorship machine.

Mr. Bancroft also suggested that the "threat of unjustified
criminal prosecution" for publishing classified material "can
be as effective a prior restraint as a pre-publication injunction."

Another fear expressed by several witnesses at the hearing
and by many writers and commentators is that attacks on the
press by government officials, such as Vice-President Agnew,
may act as a form of censorship. Senator Ervin warned that

the First Amendment did not give the press freedom from criticism, yet attacks such as those of Mr. Agnew might well muzzle the press. Reporters and editors, sensitive to a charge of bias, may well avoid legitimate criticism of government officials and even "bend over backward" to give favorable reports on government activities. There are those who believe that Mr. Agnew's attacks had exactly that result. The *New Yorker* magazine commented in February 1970, some months after Mr. Agnew's speech:

> As we have watched the news on television and read the papers since the Agnew speeches, we have had the feeling that the Administration has been allowed to assume a leading role in establishing the relative importance both of news stories and of issues. The new "fairness"—i.e., "fairness" to the Administration—has become indistinguishable from fear of the Administration. In hundreds of tiny ways, news coverage now seems to reflect an eagerness to please the people in positions of power. . . . We have an impression that the President's picture is being run more often in the papers than it used to be. In editorials, it has suddenly become popular to praise President Nixon's "effectiveness" or "adroitness" in political maneuvering, but without asking what the goals of his maneuvering are.

These "impressions" of the editors of the *New Yorker* may well not be correct. But the *New Yorker* was at least making clear the risk that attacks on press bias by influential government officials can pose a threat to the integrity of the press and its function to criticize. As a political writer for a west coast newspaper put it in a comment to *Time* magazine, "Buried in our subconscious is the thought: 'Be goddam careful. Don't start a beef.' "

Of more direct concern to journalists as a threat to press freedom is the subpoenaing of reporters and their notes by courts, grand juries, and government investigative bodies. Mr. Bancroft identified the trend:

. . . although *Times'* reporters received a total of only five subpoenaes or demands for documents in the entire period from 1964 through 1967, three were received in 1968, six in 1969, and twelve in 1970. The accelerating pace at which subpoenaes have been served on The *Times* has also been the experience of the other media. NBC, CBS and their wholly-owned affiliates, for example, in the period from 1969 through July, 1971, alone, have been served with more than 123 subpoenaes.

Can a reporter be forced against his will to reveal his sources of information and to surrender notes, documents, and other records pertinent to that information? The issue went to the Supreme Court in a case involving Earl Caldwell, a *New York Times* reporter. His stories on the Black Panther party in San Francisco prompted a federal grand jury to subpoena him and his notes. Caldwell refused to appear and his actions were upheld by the Court of Appeals. In 1972, the Supreme Court ruled that Caldwell had to testify, a decision generally decried by the press.

No issue is more important to a reporter than the protection of his news sources. He lives by honoring their confidentiality. His integrity is at stake. All sources of confidential information will stop talking to him if they believe he will or can be made to reveal their identity. More than a few reporters have gone to jail rather than reveal who told them what.

It is argued that if reporters are required to lose all confidential sources, then the public will be the ultimate loser. The immediate results may be the capture of a few criminals whom the reporter may know about, but there will also be a drying up of important sources of information about the affairs of government. Most political and governmental reporters cultivate news sources who leak news to them or offer background explanations for the events that are taking place. If all such sources of news are stopped, the public's knowledge of governmental affairs will diminish.

Yet, it is argued that a reporter has a duty to society to report the occurrence of crimes or other harmful activity. The needs of society to know what the reporter knows take precedence over that reporter's need to protect his individual sources.

Battles over censorship of the press are old in America. Each new generation of politicians finds grounds on which to attack the press for its limitations and excesses, yet, fortunately, each new generation of journalists finds the courage to fight attempts to censor one of America's essential freedoms. Indeed, reporters were jailed in Newark, New Jersey, and Los Angeles, California, in 1972 for failing to disclose sources of information.

# CHAPTER 11
# Censorship of Broadcasting

BROADCAST journalism does not have the same freedom as the nation's newspapers and magazines. The broadcast industry —particularly television—maintains that it is unjustly and dangerously censored by the government. More than a few people, on the other hand, believe television newscasting should be even more heavily censored than it is.

It is certain that television news is different from printed news and that it does receive, whether or not it should, special attention from the government and the public.

The reason for this special treatment lies in the tremendous potency of television news. It is widely believed that most Americans gain more news from television than from newspapers, and that a significant number of people rely solely upon television to learn about what is happening in the world.

Moreover, television news has tremendous impact. The viewer can sit in his living room and see and hear a battle in Vietnam, a riot in Chicago, a speech in Washington, a flood in Pennsylvania. The distant events are brought to his home and he sees them while they are happening. He can form his own impression of those events and that impression is often a highly emotional one.

Television certainly has the potential instantly to change

the nation's attitudes. It may be argued that it has already demonstrated this capacity. In 1965, television showed mounted police swinging whips and clubs charge into a group of peaceful black marchers in Selma, Alabama. The brutality of the scene shocked Americans and was instrumental in passage of voting rights legislation shortly thereafter. In 1968, a riot between police and demonstrators in the middle of the Democratic National Convention in Chicago again shocked Americans. Attitudes hardened either for or against the police. Americans have seen the murders of President Kennedy, his assassin Lee Harvey Oswald, and Senator Robert F. Kennedy on television, as well as the attempted murder of Governor George C. Wallace of Alabama. In each instance, the American people have been appalled. Deep concern about the causes of violence have resulted.

There *are* inherent dangers in television newscasting. Television is simply a much different medium from either radio or the printed word. These differences are not really understood, even within the television industry. There has been little serious study of the medium and its impact and how its advantages might be enhanced, its disadvantages minimized. The nature of the medium underlies attempts to censor television.

Television is extraordinarily fleeting. It reproduces motion picture film or tape running at the rate of sixteen frames per second. The reels run on, offering a constant stream of images. An incident or episode is shown. The viewer has time only for a quick, usually emotional impression before the next and different image appears. Serious consideration of any of what has been seen is very difficult.

By its very nature, television news must (or usually does) deal with complex matters in abbreviated form. Television has found ways to devote hours of detailed coverage to such events as men on the moon, national political conventions, presidential inaugurals, the funerals of John and Robert Kennedy, Harry S. Truman, and similar personages—not to mention sports events, Thanksgiving parades, and old movies. Yet, in its network news programs it crams the news of the day into a half hour, with part of the time allotted to commercials. The important events of the day, if they are mentioned at all, are reduced to sentences. Only the most major events can command as much as a minute of a telecast.

Some years ago when Chet Huntley and David Brinkley were doing the evening news for NBC, they had the content of a half-hour broadcast printed into the format of the *New York Times*. The entire broadcast filled only three-quarters of one page of the *Times*. Such brevity cannot possibly lead to any comprehensive presentation of the day's events or any real understanding of those items of news that are presented.

Even in its hour-long "in depth" treatments of social and political problems, television is trivial and cursory. I can give some firsthand evidence for this statement. Early in 1969, I was commissioned to write two books on the history of slavery in America based upon installments of the CBS "Of Black America" series, which had run some weeks before. One program had been highly praised and had won an Emmy Award from the industry. I viewed the program carefully. All of the CBS research materials for the program were made available to me. In all honesty, everyone, including CBS, the publisher, editors and myself, thought it would be a simple task to translate that program into a book. After all, the research had all been done.

A rather rude awakening was not long in coming. Little research had been performed by CBS News and the entire content of the program, when reduced to the printed word, consisted of only a few paragraphs at most. In essence, the program presented only a couple of concepts, each copiously illustrated. One was that Americans are unaware of black contributions to America and the second was that there is black prejudice in America and has been for a long time. The largest segment of the program, nearly half of it, consisted of film clips from old Hollywood movies, showing how black people were ridiculed and demeaned in films in the 1930s and 1940s. The next largest segment was interviews with Southerners to show racial attitudes.

There was absolutely no way to turn this utter paucity of material into one book, let alone two, purporting to be histories. It was necessary to discard all of the CBS materials and undertake an immense research task into the origins of slavery and the slave trade, the nature of slavery, and its effects on America. Such a task would be so difficult for television as to be virtually impossible. Many hours, perhaps hundreds of them, would have had to be devoted to the programs and they probably would have been very dull.

A greater problem even than brevity is the fact that television is a slave to the motion picture camera. A newscast simply cannot consist of an announcer sitting and reading the news, for that is visually uninteresting. Television must *illustrate* the news. It must have action films of people doing something or of events happening.

The content of the news program thereby is greatly determined by the illustrative film that is available. The television camera is a bulky instrument and made more so if sound is to be reproduced with it. Camera and sound men cannot be all places, no matter how hard they try. They ride the streets in radio equipped cars. They rush to a scene of an accident, perhaps to film a "fender-bender" while a fatal crash occurs across town; perhaps to film the arrest of a sneak thief, while a bank is robbed elsewhere. A senator is filmed as he emerges from the White House to make a few remarks, while somewhere else a dam breaks immersing a town. A camera crew accompanies an Army unit on a patrol in Vietnam. It has an uneventful time, while a major, untelevised battle takes place somewhere else.

There are many possible examples, all of which are unavoidable. Yet, the film that is available dictates the contents of the news. Television cameramen may be dispatched with haste to the flood, fire, battle or other event, but again the film they shoot will dictate the contents of the next day's telecast.

Television newsmen know this. They try mightily to anticipate the next day's news. Camera crews are readily available to the White House, Capitol, United Nations, and other places where news is made frequently. Television journalists have at times been remarkably successful in having cameras on hand when major events took place. The murder on television of Oswald is just one example. But no broadcast journalist would contend the record is anything but spotty.

When no film is available of an event, announcers read a brief report of it. But again, the entire program cannot consist of the reading of such reports, even if illustrated with still pictures of the event. Unfortunately, the limitations of illustrative film force newscasters to allot an undue portion of the brief time available to less important, even trivial news. There then follows a natural tendency to make the unimportant seem more important than it really is. The uneventful Army patrol is made typical or a microcosm of the nature of the war. The senatorial remarks at the door of the White House are cited as evidence of important actions by the president.

The perhaps unconscious elevation of the trivial is but one way that television *makes* news rather than simply reports it. This is a most serious and frequently heard charge. Many people have observed that the mere appearance of a camera and sound crew at the scene of a disturbance leads people to begin to act so as to attract the cameraman's attention. There are several documented instances when the arrival of the camera worsened or even precipitated a riot.

Television has had a serious effect on the forms of dissent in America. Many dissenters, eager to make their views known to the public, have sought to make use of television by providing action for the camera to film. The protests or demonstrations are planned and announced so the cameras are at hand. Rather than simply reading a prepared statement, the demonstrators march up and down, carry placards, sing or make noise, and even bait the police to cause violence. It is a serious charge to make that television provokes violence in America, but not one wholly without a basis in fact.*

* For a fuller treatment of the effects of television on dissent, read the author's *Dissent in America,* (New York: McGraw-Hill, N.Y., 1971).

One other inherent danger in television news must be mentioned. To be on television is a tremendous lure to many people. Newspaper reporters have long observed the eagerness of some individuals to get their name or photograph in the paper. The success of radio talk shows indicates the enthusiasm of people to get on the air. But these phenomena pale beside the eagerness of people to be seen on television. Consider only the frantic waving of spectators at sporting events when a camera is pointed in their direction or the actions of the studio audience when shown on an entertainment program.

Such antics are certainly harmless. But it is at least arguable that this harmless phenomenon becomes more serious when the demented in our society, thirsting for any sort of recognition and notoriety in their wretched lives, take gun in hand to stalk celebrities. It is certainly a subject worthy of serious study to determine to what extent if any the desire to get on television and become famous motivated Oswald to murder President Kennedy, Sirhan Sirhan to kill Senator Kennedy, and Arthur Bremer to attempt to assassinate Governor Wallace.

In no sense, can this be construed to mean that television is responsible for political assassinations or violence in America. But with study it might be possible to prove or disprove that an inherent danger of the television medium is that it offers an irresistable lure to unstable minds desperate for attention and recognition.

Television is simply a far different medium for news than either radio or the printed word. This has led to a number of efforts, both governmental and private, to control it and minimize its dangers—in a word censor television news.

First let us consider private actions in this direction. Television newsmen are acutely aware of their responsibility. An eloquent statement of industry attitudes was made by Walter Cronkite, CBS News correspondent, to the Ervin subcommittee in the Senate:

Vice President Agnew was right in asserting that a handful of us determine what will be on the evening news broadcast. . . .

Indeed, it is a handful of us with this awesome power— power that not one of us underestimates or takes lightly. It is a strongly editorial power. With each time we report we can and do seek factual honesty, fairness and balance. But we must decide *which* [his emphasis] news items out of hundreds available we are going to expose that day. And those available to us already have been culled and re-culled by persons far outside our control. The local newspaper, let us say the *Kansas City Star,* decides each day which of the events of its area it will cover. The local press service representative, AP, or UPI, decides which of those items will go onto his wire. A regional relay editor decides which of the items on the regional wire shall go on to New York or Washington or Los Angeles. And we decide which of those items remaining are to go on the air. In the case of television, the decision frequently involves which items will be illustrated by film—which we freely acknowledge gives the item far greater impact than the paragraph recited by the broadcaster. And film choice, in a sense, also may be taken out of our hands by technical considerations —fogged films, unintelligible sound tract, a dozen things can go wrong.

Many factors go into the decision we make, so many and so complex that it would be hopeless to attempt to detail them here.

With the difficulty of proving a negative, I cannot in any way produce evidence to support the next statement. I can only give you my personal assurance—and what that is worth is only as much as you judge my veracity—I assure you that I have never heard nor guessed nor felt that the news judgment in making any one of those decisions was based on a political or ideological consideration. Not one I believe, I trust, that my colleagues at the other networks can say the same.

Now let me repeat, since I am not entirely naïve, I do know that, like an insidious, tasteless, odorless gas, prejudice and bias can sneak in and poison the decision-making process. But like a fireman in a smoke-filled room, a deep-sea diver with the first symptoms of narcosis, a surgeon with a second-sense that the patient is failing under his hands, we *feel* [his emphasis] the creeping danger and most of the time—not always because we are not perfect—we react and we bend over backwards to regain balance in the report.

Mr. Cronkite did more than simply ask for trust in his and other newscasters' judgment. He made essentially the same arguments as print journalists that freedom of information and public participation in the democracy depends on freedom of the press, including broadcast journalism.

He also maintained that there is no suitable alternative to the editorial functions of the working broadcaster. Who could do it better? His argument deserves to be quoted at some length:

> We would never get on the air or go to press if we attempted to submit each judgment to a committee of Congressmen, bureaucrats, sociologists, teachers, policemen, union leaders, women liberationists. Nor can we go to a plebiscite for each decision.
>
> No one is suggesting, as far as I know, that ludicrous thought. There are those, however, who proposed ex post facto examination of the journalists' judgment. This, on the surface, may seem innocuous enough. Far from it! It would be as effective a clamp on press freedom as direct censorship.
>
> Any government panel that presumes to call a news organization to account for its actions must be presumed to be hostile. It scarcely would seek to investigate reporting with which it agreed.
>
> To place the licensed broadcast medium under the threat of such investigation is to place it permanently under the fear of accountability to unfriendly antagonists wielding the power of legal restraint.
>
> The effect would be more chilling on broadcast reporting. It would put journalistic enterprise in the deep freeze, with the rigidity and the heart and compassion of a block of ice.
>
> Rare, indeed, would be the station or network management willing to commit unlimited resources of its legal and executive staff to defend a documentary or daily reportage when it would be far more comfortable simply to forego mention of the item or the subject.
>
> Impossible would be the position of the journalist working under such understandably timid management. For each piece of potentially controversial reporting (and there is scarcely any topic, including the weather, that is *not* controversial) he

would presumably have to go to management for approval to broadcast.

Or, since this would be impractical, he would ignore the item and fill his broadcast with something less likely to involve his company and himself in lengthy review by non-professional and frequently politically biased critics.

There is no question here of whether the reporters and editors perform well or poorly, with accuracy or inaccuracy, or even, with objectivity or with bias. The question is whether those who are elected to public office on partisan platforms, who represent, properly, the special interests of their region, who by their political nature properly hold strong views on the issues of the day, should be vested with the right to say whether broadcast journalism is performing in the people's interests. They certainly are qualified to define these interests in *their* lights, but it clearly would be unjust and fatal to press freedom for them to sit in judgment on the men and women who are reporting the manner in which *they* discharge their public responsibilities.

Mr. Cronkite pointed out that newspapers are "severe critics" of the broadcast medium, suggesting there is "adequate check and balance" between the competing media.

To deny the free play of these forces by putting one of them under the surveillance of government would be to deny the people a balance between media that can assure a free press.

The fears of broadcasters such as Walter Cronkite are more real than imaginary, for all radio and television stations are licensed and regulated by the federal government through the Federal Communications Commission (FCC).

Virtually to a man, broadcasters abhor the regulation, consider it harmful and unnecessary and a means of censorship. To quote Cronkite again:

Broadcast news today is not free. Because it is operated by an industry that is beholden to the government for its right to exist, its freedom has been curtailed by fiat, by assumption, and by intimidation and harassment.

The Ervin subcommittee heard testimony from Mr. Cronkite and from Dr. Frank Stanton, president of CBS. Both men railed at the FCC, citing a long list of complaints that they contended are indirect censorship. The subcommittee also heard from Dean Burch, chairman, and Nicholas Johnson, member, of the FCC. They offered explanations of the commission's work and rulings, the legal basis for its functions, the need for it to continue to function, and the role the commission plays in guaranteeing both freedom of the press and information. To read these four statements, so opposite are their contentions, is to wonder if the four were talking about the same subject. We can search for a reasonable conclusion by presenting the various points of view on the more controversial issues.

The first issue is whether or not there is a need for federal licensing. Such licensing dates to the early days of radio in 1927. There were and are only a limited number of radio frequencies and television channels. Mr. Burch called these a "precious, scarce resource" that must be reserved as part of the public domain and used for the public benefit.

The Supreme Court has twice upheld the licensing of broadcasting stations. In 1942, in *NBC v. U.S.,* it ruled:

> Freedom of utterance is abridged to any who wish to use the limited facilities of radio. Unlike other modes of expression, radio inherently is not available to all. That is its unique characteristic and that is why unlike other modes of expression, it is subject to government regulation.

In the *Red Lion* decision of 1969, the Court again ruled:

> Where there are substantially more individuals who want to broadcast than there are frequencies to allocate, it is idle to posit an unabridgeable First Amendment right to broadcast comparable to the right of every individual to speak, write or publish.

A perhaps clearer statement was made by Chief Justice Warren Burger in 1966, when he was a member of the Court of Appeals in Washington, D.C.:

> A broadcaster has much in common with a newspaper publisher, but he is not in the same category in terms of public obligations imposed by law. A broadcaster seeks and is granted the free exclusive use of a limited and valuable part of the public domain, when he accepts that franchise, it is burdened by enforceable public obligations. A newspaper can be operated at the whim or caprice of its owners; a broadcast station cannot. After nearly five decades of operation, the broadcast industry does not seem to have grasped the simple fact that a broadcast license is a public trust subject to termination for breach of duty.

The broadcast industry mounts some counterarguments. Since the opening of the FM radio bands, there are now so many radio stations in operation, offering such a variety of programming, that there is no need to license any of them. There are fewer television stations, but nearly every city has unused channels because they cannot be operated profitably. Said Mr. Cronkite:

> The doctrine that the air belongs to the people because broadcast channels are a rare natural resource is today largely myth. The myth is further exposed by the advent of cable television. The wired cities of tomorrow (there are, of course, some today)—not using the "people's air" at all—will have an almost unlimited number of channels available.

Licensing in itself probably would not disturb broadcasters so much were it not for the regulation that accompanies it. Again Cronkite commented upon this:

> The FCC has interpreted that right to examine a station's programming, to require a certain portion of time to be allotted to so-called public affairs programming, to provide rebuttal under the fairness and equal time doctrines.

Tribute should be paid to the wisdom of Federal Communications Commission members, past and present, that the regulatory body had not gone further. But the power to make us conform is too great to forever lie dormant. The axe lies there temptingly for the use of any enraged administration— Republican, Democrat, Wallacite or McCarthyite. We are at the mercy of the whim of politicians and bureaucrats and whether they choose to chop us down or not, the mere existence of their power is an intimidating and constraining threat in being.

The Act of Congress setting up the FCC specifically prohibited it from censoring broadcasting stations. Mr. Burch confirmed the commission's devotion to the prohibition in describing how the FCC enforces its regulations against deliberate distortion or slanting of the news.

. . . we may get a complaint of new distortion based on the claim that the facts of some matter are different from those presented over the air. We have absolutely refused to act there. Very simply stated, deliberate distortion cannot be established by determining what is "true" and then comparing it with what was broadcast. The Commission is not the national arbiter of "truth." Similarly, when a person quoted on a news program complains that he very clearly said something else, the Commission cannot investigate and weigh the credibility of the newsman and the interviewed party. We refer the matter to the licensee for its own investigation and appropriate handling. . . .

In every case where we may appropriately do so—where there is, for example, extrinsic evidence that a newsman has been directed to slant the news—we shall act to protect the public interest in a responsible press. But in this democracy, no government agency can, or should try, to authenticate the news. Therefore, in a series of recent cases we have consistently and repeatedly stated that we will shun the censor's role and will not try to establish news distortion in situations where government intervention would constitute a worse danger than the possible rigging itself.

CBS itself became involved in a case of alleged distortion, not with the FCC but with the House Committee on Interstate and Foreign Commerce, chaired by Representative Harley O. Staggers of West Virginia. At issue was the news documentary "The Selling of the Pentagon," which was telecast on February 23 and March 23, 1971. The program dealt with the public-relations activities of the Department of Defense.

Charges of distortion in the program were based on two episodes in the program. First, it was charged that answers given by Assistant Defense Secretary Daniel Z. Henkin were mismatched with the questions he had been asked. In other words, he gave those answers, but not to those questions. Second, a speech by Lieutenant Colonel John MacNeil was cut up and rearranged so that six widely disconnected and insequential sentences were made to appear as if they had been delivered successively without interruption.

The Staggers committee asked for outtakes or unedited film for the program. CBS refused to provide them. Dr. Stanton, CBS president, was subpoenaed to appear before the committee with the outtakes. He again refused, defending his action under Freedom of the Press. The committee voted to hold Dr. Stanton in contempt of Congress, but the entire House membership voted not to bring the charge against Dr. Stanton. The vote occurred at the time when freedom of the press was a national issue because of the court cases involving the Pentagon Papers.

The major source of disagreement between the FCC and the broadcast industry involves the so-called "fairness doctrine" of the FCC. Mr. Burch described it to the Ervin subcommittee:

> Simply stated, the fairness doctrine requires that where a broadcaster has covered one side of a controversial issue of public importance, he must afford reasonable opportunity for the discussion of contrasting viewpoints. He cannot sit back and wait for someone to knock on his door and offer to present the other side. He must affirmatively encourage and implement the presentation of other sides—by making offers

over-the-air or to specific groups of persons representing other
viewpoints. In presenting other viewpoints the broadcaster has
considerable leeway to make good faith, reasonable judgments
as to the viewpoints to be presented, the appropriate spokesmen, the format of the program, and many other similar programming decisions. Thus fairness, that is, affording "reasonable" opportunity does not mean the mathematical precision
of "equal" opportunities—a concept which is applicable only
to broadcasts by legally qualified candidates.

The commission's role in enforcing the fairness doctrine is
limited. The commission determines, upon appropriate complaint, whether the broadcaster's judgment can be said to be
unreasonable. The commission does not, I stress, determine
whether it is a wise journalistic judgment or one with which
this agency would agree.

Dr. Stanton sharply criticized the FCC's handling of the
doctrine.

. . . today more than at any time in the history of radio and
television, broadcast journalism is jeopardized by attempts to
regulate its content or its methods, including unreasonable ap-
plication of the FCC's fairness doctrine to the coverage of
controversial public issues. In the past, CBS has had no difficulty with that doctrine because it reflected our basic journalistic goal—to present public issues fairly. Recently, however, in
considering fairness doctrine complaints, the commission has
engaged in microscopic examination of a licensee's coverage of
an issue, going to such extremes as counting of lines in a
broadcast transcript.

Dr. Stanton gave examples. He said the commission considered twenty-eight pages of correspondence over a five
month period before deciding that a nine-minute feature on
bullfighting did not constitute a controversial issue justifying a
request for "equal time." A Miami station was found to have
violated the fairness doctrine in its coverage of a proposal for
legalization of casino gambling. Said Dr. Stanton:

. . . the commission actually counted the lines of copy devoted to both sides of the issue and apparently relied on the line count in making its decision that the station should have presented more pro-gambling material.

A more serious incident mentioned by Dr. Stanton was the CBS attempt to begin a Loyal Opposition series. The concept was that the president, be he Democrat or Republican, has a unique advantage when he commandeers television to address the nation. No member of the opposition has a comparable pulpit to counter the presidential views. After a series of nationwide television talks by President Nixon, CBS offered a single free broadcast to the Democratic National Committee to reply to or to criticize or to endorse the president's statements. On complaint from the Republican National Committee, the FCC held that the Republicans were entitled to a reply to the Democrats—"a reply, in other words, to a reply," as Dr. Stanton expressed it. The issue has dragged through the courts and the important television concept has come to naught. The "public is the loser," Dr. Stanton said.

It is not difficult to understand why broadcasters are so vehement in their opposition to the fairness doctrine. It is simply insulting to them. The doctrine attempts to impose by bureaucratic fiat a principle that ranks high in the code of ethics of professional journalists. They seek to be fair. They will be judged by their colleagues, as well as their readers or their listeners, on the basis of their fairness in presenting information. Reviewers of books, articles, and broadcasts will sharply criticize them for being unfair and warn others that they are unfair. The broadcasters argue that the fairness doctrine is simply unnecessary. Corollaries would be for the government to regulate doctors to see that they seek to cure disease, lawyers to see that they defend their clients, engineers that they build sound structures, artists that they try to enlarge the meaning of life, scientists that they seek evidence of the operation of natural processes.

It may be further argued that fairness is objectively indefinable. No man can decide, and all men can disagree when the proper degree of fairness has been reached. It is similar to trying to define obscenity.

Finally, there are several issues in American life where fairness is patently undesirable. It is difficult to imagine a television network being required to give a half hour or whatever of "equal time" to advocates of racial or religious prejudice, the American Nazi party, those who would overthrow the government by assassinating the president or bombing Congress. It is difficult to imagine a defense on television of pollution or war or crime. Should the fairness doctrine be extended to those who enjoy pornography, advocates of free love, child beaters, and mainliners of heroin? Should members of the organized criminal rackets be given equal time to defend free enterprise in murder and pillage?

The fairness doctrine, no matter how wisely enforced by the FCC, is censorship. The only question is whether or not the nation wants or needs it.

# CHAPTER 12
# The Last Word

AMERICA has experienced a great deal of dissent in recent years. There have been protests, demonstrations, and more than a little violence over such issues as the war in Vietnam, racial inequality, women's rights, pollution.

Young people have been in the forefront of the dissent. They are challenging "The System" and criticizing "The Establishment." They voice a gross dissatisfaction with America, her methods, and her goals. They want her to be better to love her the more. Such attitudes have perhaps inevitably led to clashes with other Americans who believe that the United States, faults and all, is better than most or all other countries. They say "my country—right or wrong" and "America—love it or leave it."

The result of all this has been years of turmoil, strife, polarization of ideas, confusion, a national malaise featuring indecision and lack of will. In many ways, we resemble an international psychiatric case with a diagnosis of schizophrenia.

Although there are many who would describe the condition in America differently, it must be agreed that America is undergoing a difficult period.

There are perhaps as many causes for the American malaise as there are people to suggest them. But censorship is certainly one of the root causes in America.

We do have such censorship—a great deal of it. It is insidious and pervasive. There is so much censorship of information, both public and private, that we are seldom aware of it all and tend to take it for granted. As we have seen, bureaucrats, great and petty, almost routinely stamp "top secret" and "secret" labels on government documents with personal whim being a pronounced reason for doing so. Government officials use a variety of means to try to "manage" the news. Information is withheld or released for greatest impact on public thinking. A large amount of political self-serving seems to be a motive for the process.

The mass media in America is censored. The censorship results from government classification, regulation—particularly of broadcasting—and occasional intimidation. Other censorship of the press is generated internally through the efforts of advertisers, owners, and codes of ethics.

What are the advantages of such censorship? Most of it occurs in the name of "national security" and "national unity," as well as "good taste," "editorial judgment," and "responsibility." All these considerations may well be valid, but it certainly is debatable if, as a result of such censorship, Americans feel particularly secure and have heightened unity.

A more cogent reason for the censorship lies in our form of government and the difficulty America has in forming a majority opinion and having that majority act. It is too large a subject for this book, but if the thesis of Professor Neustadt (discussed in Chapter 10) is correct, the American president is almost duty bound to try to manage the news so as to form public support for his policies so that he can get them enacted and carried out. The American form of government, as presently constituted, may well require such forms of censorship to function effectively.

An extremely serious ramification of censorship of information is that it leads to government by governors, rather than government by the governed. The American dream has always been democracy, that we as a people are wise enough to govern ourselves through our elected representatives. By its very nature, censorship inhibits that process by denying to the people the information they need to make a wise decision. They are left largely with the role of ratifying through the election process that which the governors have done or convinced the majority of the people they have done. It is certain that Americans might have reached a different decision in the mid-1960s, if they had known the information revealed in the Pentagon Papers in 1971.

Is government by governors inevitable? We are not a pure democracy in which the people rule directly, passing and administering laws. We are too large and populated a nation for that. There is too great a need for the government to act speedily and decisively. We are thereby a republic, with government by representatives of the people.

There are instant problems with such a system. The federal government alone consists of about 3 million civilian employees and over 2 million soldiers and sailors. Of this massive number, exactly 537 are elected by the people—100 senators, 435 representatives, one president and one largely powerless vice-president. For so few to control so many in the name of the people is extraordinarily difficult under the best of circumstances. When censorship of information is invoked, such control drifts toward the impossible. We are left, as a people in this republic, to rely on the goodwill, wisdom, and public spiritedness of millions of bureaucrats who are, to use the parlance, "doing God knows what."

A few of the results surface to public knowledge. The military, backed by the president, plan a secret and daring raid on a prisoner-of-war camp in North Vietnam. With great courage, the troops helicopter in, but find no Americans to liberate. The officers are brought to the White House to be personally decorated by President Nixon for their bravery in accomplishing nothing. In the background a member of the president's staff tells *Newsweek* magazine, "We are merchandising what remains one big flop." The commander of a Coast Guard vessel permits Russian sailors to board the ship to overpower and bind a Russian sailor who had sought asylum on American territory. The commander of the American Air Force in Vietnam ignores his orders and bombs North Vietnam because he personally believes it is necessary. The FBI conducts, on its own, secret surveillance of members of various dissenting and minority groups.

Another argument is made on behalf of censorship, that the nature of governmental affairs has become so complex that it is beyond the understanding of ordinary men and even the expert. Such matters as economics, international finance, taxation, military procurement, research and development, pollution control—to name but a few—have become so complicated, so much a matter for specialized expertise, that few Americans can follow them, let alone make wise judgments in these matters. Walter Lippmann, the distinguished journalist and writer, was among those who cited these complexities as a cause of our becoming a nation of the governed. The United States Senate lost its role as a forum for debate, in his view, because the senators do not know enough about complex matters to debate them intelligently.

Perhaps. But there is another line of argument. The United States government does not have a monopoly on expertise. Universities and business concerns contain people who are expert in the complex and obtuse. If they had full information on what the government is doing, they could formulate ideas and communicate them to the public. Moreover, the most obtuse can be made simple so that the nonexpert can understand it, if sincere effort is made. Albert Einstein could explain his theory of relativity to a child. Doctors routinely manage to convey the intricacies of medicine to their patients. If the people wish to participate in the affairs of government, at least by knowing what has taken place, they can participate, expertise be damned.

Censorship simply makes participation in democratic government more difficult than it needs to be. Censorship also has one other effect which needs to be mentioned here. It leads to a concept of government as benefiting the *nation* rather than the *people*.

There is a difference. We regularly make protestations of our friendship for the Russian and the Chinese people, while abhorring their totalitarian forms of government. The Russian and Chinese leaders do the same, saying how much they like Americans, but not the American government. There is a risk that censorship can lead to government by governors who act for the benefit of the nation rather than the people.

It is said the war in Vietnam has benefited the nation by preserving our influence in Southeast Asia, limiting the spread of communism, and bolstering the South Vietnamese nation. Even if all this is granted, then it is at least debatable whether that long, slow war in Vietnam has benefited the American people in any short- or long-range way.

The nation may benefit from America's multibillion dollar annual expenditure for an international spying apparatus, but it is difficult to figure exactly what this does for the American people. The quartering of troops in Europe, South Korea, and scores of other places around the world may contribute, as is maintained, to our nation's role in world affairs, but it is hard to assess exactly what benefit the American people receive for this sacrifice of manpower and money.

Americans believe, because we live in a democracy, that we are indivisible as a nation and as a people. Because of censorship of information, there is at least a risk of division. When embarrassing facts are hidden behind a top-secret stamp, when a bureaucrat decides on his own that certain facts should be hidden from the public, when government agencies charge a high dollar price to provide information legitimately requested by the people, when even Congress cannot learn certain information, when federal agents maintain secret wiretaps, when detailed information about millions of citizens is stored in computers for possible use in the future, when . . . when . . . when—then we are entertaining a risk at least of government by governors for the benefit of governors—and, to paraphrase Abraham Lincoln, government *for* the people rather than *by* or *of* the people.

When causes for the unrest and dissatisfaction in America are sought, the use of censorship of information to preclude participation in government must rank as a major cause.

Censorship is as old as the nation. It is insidious. It is self-serving and self-perpetuating. It has also been fought by every generation of Americans. Hopefully the new generation of young people now moving into the seats of power will not fail to carry on the struggle for freedom of information.

# Selected Reading

Ernst, Morris L. and Schwartz, Alan U. *Censorship: The Search for the Obscene.* New York: Macmillan, 1964.

Haney, Robert W. *Comstockery in America.* Boston: Beacon Press, 1960.

Hoyt, Olga and Edwin P. *Censorship in America.* New York: Seabury Press, 1970.

Kilpatrick, James Jackson. *The Smut Peddlers.* Garden City, N.Y.: Doubleday, 1960.

McClellan, Grand S., ed. *Censorship in the United States.* New York: H. W. Wilson Co., 1967.

Moon, Eric, ed. *Book Selection and Censorship in the Sixties.* New York: R. R. Bowker, 1969.

Murphy, Terrence J. *Censorship: Government and Obscenity.* Baltimore: Helicon Press, 1963.

Paul, James C. N. and Schwartz, Murray L. *Federal Censorship.* New York: The Free Press of Glencoe, 1961.

Randall, Richard S. *Censorship of the Movies.* Madison, Wisc.: The University of Wisconsin Press, 1968.

Rembar, Charles. *The End of Obscenity.* New York: Random House, 1968.

Rosenberg, Jerry M. *The Death of Privacy.* New York: Random House, 1969.

# Index